Library of
Davidson College

THE STANZAIC *MORTE*

A Verse Translation of *Le Morte Arthur*

Sharon Kahn

UNIVERSITY
PRESS OF
AMERICA

THE STANZAIC MORTE

A Verse Translation of *Le Morte Arthur*

Sharon Kahn

UNIVERSITY
PRESS OF
AMERICA

LANHAM • NEW YORK • LONDON

Copyright © 1986 by

University Press of America,® Inc.

4720 Boston Way
Lanham, MD 20706

3 Henrietta Street
London WC2E 8LU England

All rights reserved

Printed in the United States of America

Library of Congress Cataloging in Publication Data

Morte Arthur.
   The stanzaic morte.

   Bibliography: p.
   1. Arthurian romances.   I. Kahn, Sharon.   II. Title.
PR2065.M5A34   1986   821'.1   86-9175
ISBN 0-8191-5426-1 (alk. paper)
ISBN 0-8191-5427-X (pbk. : alk. paper)

All University Press of America books are produced on acid-free
paper which exceeds the minimum standards set by the National
Historical Publications and Records Commission.

CONTENTS

INTRODUCTION

    Arthurian Literature and the Middle Ages   v

    Le Morte Arthur and the Fall of Man   vi

    The Translation   xiii

    The Story of Le Morte Arthur   xiii

LE MORTE ARTHUR   1

BIBLIOGRAPHY   124

INTRODUCTION

Arthurian Literature and the Middle Ages

The origins of King Arthur and the tales surrounding him extend so far back in the mists of time that scholars today can verify little about them other than the likelihood that someone bearing the name of Arthur may possibly have existed in early Britain. The military exploits of a dux bellorum, or war leader, are mentioned as early as the sixth century in Gildas' De Excido Britanniae, and these acts are later attributed to an Arthur by Nennius in his ninth century Historia Brittonum. From the time of these early historical references until today, stories of Arthur and his knights have grown to phenomenal proportions, experiencing their greatest growth during the Middle Ages. These tales incorporated a grain of historical truth, components of Celtic legend, classic mythology, and French folktales, as well as elements of medieval Christianity and considerable amounts of magic and superstition. It is difficult to say why an obscure battle-lord should come to play such a large role in the literature of the Western world. It can only be assumed that the growth of his fame and popularity owe much to tradition and circumstance of which we have no knowledge today.

Much of what we consider to be English and Arthurian comes to us by way of France, for it was from there that the Matter of Britain, as it was called, spread through the Low Countries, Denmark, Germany, Switzerland, Bohemia and Portugal. By the twelfth century, the stories that made up the Arthurian cycle had achieved as great a popularity in England as they had on the continent. Versions of these tales originally passed along by storytellers and troubadors were now written down pretty much in the form that we recognize today. Chrétien de Troyes consolidated much of the Arthurian material and became a major influence on many of the later writers, both French and English.

Towards the close of the Middle Ages, however, the popularity of Arthurian tales began to wane. Although they were never to lose popularity entirely, the Renaissance with its new ways of looking at man and his world, and its new styles of expressing the emotions of a new era began to bring the golden age of Arthur to its close, which was climaxed by William Caxton's publication of Sir Thomas Malory's Le Morte Darthur in 1485.

It is Malory's version of the Arthurian stories that encompass what we today are likely to have in mind when we think of Arthurian legend. But Malory, of course, drew upon earlier sources for his works, primarily the French romances, and quite possibly, in part, two fourteenth century versions of the death of Arthur, the Alliterative Morte Arthure and the Stanzaic Le Morte

Arthur. Malory's account of Arthur's death and the events leading up to it, in fact, closely resemble the account found i the Stanzaic Morte. This similarity has led some Arthuria scholars to the conclusion that the Morte was indeed the sourc for Malory's account, while others claim that any resemblance between the two can be attributed to the use of a similar source the French Mort Artu. In either case, the similarities betwee the two works make a look at the Stanzaic Morte worthwhile.

This work may be found today in the British Museum as Harle Manuscript 2252. It is generally agreed that it was written dow around 1400 in the Northern Midlands of England. The poem consists of 3,969 lines divided into stanzas of eight four beat line rhymed alternately, with two rhyming sounds to each stanza. page of the manuscript is missing, as are, perhaps, seven pairs o lines in other parts of the poem where stanzas exist that lack th full eight lines found elsewhere.

The tale is presented in the style of the minstrel romanc ballad and often contains many of the formulas common to tha style. It presents, nevertheless, a quickly moving narrativ dealing with the adulterous love of Lancelot and Guinever (calle Gaynor in the poem), the ill-fated love of the Maid of Ascolat fo Lancelot, the treachery of Mordred and the other events that le to the fateful battle that was to result in Arthur's death and th destruction of his kingdom.

Le Morte Arthur and the Fall of Man

Le Morte Arthur, the Stanzaic Morte, is significant, not onl because it was possibly one of the sources used by Malory for L Morte Darthur, but because it is an excellent example of what made that part of the Arthurian legend that deals with the las days of Arthur and his kingdom so popular.

The Stanzaic Morte contains many of the elements that appea throughout Arthurian literature, for during the Middle Ages, man versions of the story of Arthur and his court dealt primarily wit the death of the king and the events leading to it. The frequenc with which the use of this part of Arthurian lore arises at thi time may be explained by the emphasis then given to certain as pects of the legend that exemplified the manner in which medieva man may have seen the world. By the time the Stanzaic Morte wa written, the tales of the events leading to Arthur's death ha become closely interwoven with the strands of Christianity tha permeated almost every aspect of the social fabric that comprise the Western world. The Death of Arthur seemed to offer much op portunity for comment, either subtle or explicit, on the ways i which man should live.

While, as evidenced by the minstrel style of the Morte, its prime purpose was, most likely, to entertain, it also contains evidence of the fascination that its audience had with the consideration of man's role in a God-centered universe. Although not emphasized in a manner that detracts from that which had made the story popular throughout the years, a moral lesson is apparent, elements of which had began to appear in earlier versions of Arthur's death, and the incorporation of these into the Stanzaic Morte indicates the importance this message had assumed by the time the Stanzaic poet produced his poem.

The Stanzaic Morte is a good example of medieval thought in its blending of myth and tradition with Christian doctrine. Although little of the matter that makes up the poem is original, the French Mort Artu being the source for much of it, the reuse of this material shows the popularity of the fusion of intriguing story with religious moral, presenting through its use of material that suggests the Book of Genesis, the story of man's first Fall.

In its depiction of the last days of Arthur's realm, the poem's prevailing mood is one of impending disaster in the picture it presents of a society, once near perfect, but now on the path to complete destruction, not through the vagaries of fortune or fate, but through the fault of man. What the poet has borrowed from his predecessors and what he has chosen to stress show his intent. His concentration on the people involved in the tragedy, and on the events of the court, rather than on the heroics of the battle scenes that often figure strongly in accounts of Arthur's death, indicate that his main concern is to show a society moving, because of human error to the point where a futile struggle for its existence must ensue.

The Stanzaic Morte shows the futility of this struggle, letting us see how the disaster with which the poem culminates is brought about by a series of deliberate actions on the part of the people involved and by a series of unplanned accidents. For fate or accident does play a part in the tale, but it is not fate that is as much to be blamed for the eventual outcome as is man himself. It is man whose freely made choices form the pattern that the future will take. This pattern, dictated of course, by the Arthurian legend itself, is presented without any evident moralizing or pointing out of possible implications. Still, through the adventure and romance of the poem, the story of the first Fall and its attendant moral lesson begins to be seen.

Just as in the Bible story, this fall is brought about by man himself. Using the God-granted power of free-will, man again makes the choices that lead to the destruction of the ideal. Just as the choices made by Adam and Eve led to disaster, so too do those made by the characters in the Morte. The relationship between Genesis and the <u>Morte</u> is confirmed by the use of two major biblical symbols, the apple and the serpent. The influence these two have on the action of the poem serves as a reminder that we are again witnessing the events of the first Fall. But while these symbols make us aware that the territory in the <u>Morte</u> is in truth that of the Garden of Eden, it is the actions of the inhabitants of the <u>Morte</u>'s world that are shown to play as important a part as they did in the original story.

The people of the poem are confronted, as were Adam and Eve by choices, and they freely make their decisions. It is unfortunate that these decisions, dictated by emotions rooted in lust jealousy, anger or resentment, are the wrong ones and those that allow evil to breed and gain strength, and that lead to the overall pollution that in turn leads only to disaster.

The title of the poem, <u>Le Morte Arthur,</u> is the description of that disaster, Arthur's death symbolizing the fall of an earthly kingdom that came close to providing for man the sort of idyllic existence that had been found in Eden before the Fall. However it is not Arthur, primarily, whose actions and choices bring about this second Fall. In some respects, he is the representation of the God of the Old Testament. The often repeated description of him, "The kinge stode on a toure on highte," not only indicates his somewhat heavenly location, but also his separation from the motivations of mankind in the world far below him. He is the Lord to whom obedience and love are to be given unquestioningly.

It is Lancelot who, more than any of the other characters represents Adam. He, as Adam was, is confronted with the choices and it is his decisions that gradually lead to the disaster. It is Lancelot's tragedy that he is a good man and a good knight. He is, indeed, as Arthur describes him:

> Of alle the worlde the beste knight
> Off biaute and of bounte,
> And sithe is none so moche of myght
> At every dede best is he; (SM lines 123-126)

He is aware of his sin against his lord, but his love for Gaynor who of course, represents Eve, has become stronger than the love and duty owed to Arthur. His love, as did Adam's love for Eve leads to disobedience to God and a pervasion of the natural order

Lancelot's attempts to give up Gaynor and their love had led to a four year self-exile from Arthur's court, but no sooner does he return than his first action, and that first recorded in the poem, is to forsake his duty to Arthur by making excuses to remain with the queen when Arthur and most of the court leave for the tournament. This decision of Lancelot's at the opening of the poem is the first of a series of decisions, invariably the wrong ones, which Lancelot makes. In this case, his choosing to remain at home allows Agravayne, whose desire is "to take them wyth the dede," (SM 63) to further garner the evidence against Lancelot and Gaynor that he in his malice will eventually reveal to Arthur. This first choice that Lancelot makes, motivated by his love for the queen as opposed to his duty to his sovereign, will lead to the eventual fall of the realm.

Lancelot's ensuing choices are no more indicative of good results than his first one. Whenever presented with the opportunity to choose the right way, he freely chooses that which is most likely to lead to serious trouble. Given the opportunity to give up his illicit love for Gaynor for the pure and innocent love offered to him by the Maid of Ascolat, his decision is to remain in his sinful situation. He is, if anything faithful, and it is ironic that his fidelity and the other admirable qualities he possesses, become the means to make his decisions the wrong ones. It is the kindness and compassion that he feels for the Maid, suffering for love of him, that dictates his decision to wear her sleeve in the tournament and to leave his armor with her. Here too, the choice is wrong, for it is this that leads to Gaynor's hurt resentment, and to Lancelot's subsequent departure from the court. It is, to a large extent, the decisions made by Lancelot regarding the Maid of Ascolat that cause the possibility of the dissolution of Arthur's realm to become a certainty. The ill-will towards the queen, engendered by her responsibility for Lancelot's departure, turns quickly into a general atmosphere of disloyalty and strife within the court, which the knights correctly recognize as having stemmed from the relationship between Lancelot and Gaynor.

> 'Alas,' they seyd, 'launcelot du lake,
> That euyr shuldistow se the quene!' (SM 796-797)

This is, of course, the crux of the story. Lancelot's love for the queen can only lead to disaster because that love is a wrongful one, and any choices based upon it will, almost by definition, be wrongful also. These choices, possibly not wrong of themselves, are, in the frame of their context, in opposition to God's will. The use of free-will to oppose God is certain to be disastrous for man, and this is indeed the result of Lancelot's abdication of his loyalty and obedience to his king, for his failure causes Arthur's Eden, the kingdom, to weaken. And it is this weakening that permits the evil force that first manifested itself in the temptation of Lancelot and Gaynor to further increase in an atmosphere congenial to its growth, one which will allow it to develop the power to bring about the destruction its malevolent nature seeks. This is evidenced by the changing attitudes of the members of the court. Respect for the king's author-

ity and feelings of camaraderie, once the cornerstone of Arthur
fellowship erode. Once honorable knights plot to prove treaso
against the king by his queen and his most trusted friend, mor
for the sake of causing dissension and for personal ambition tha
for any moral cause, and friend slays friend in passions of ange
and resentment.

As events move inexorably out of man's control, evidence c
the workings of an unrestrained evil force can be seen moving int
operation, using various agents to perform its work. The firs
clue that we are given of this is the incident of the poisone
apple. The squire who has put the apple within Gaynor's reach i
a strangely anonymous figure. Little is told of him other than:

> With a poyson that he hath wrought
> To slay Gawayne, yif that he mighte
> In frute he hath it forthe brought
> And sette by-fore the quene bright,
> An appille ouereste lay on lofte
> There the poyson was indighte. (SM 842-847)

No reason is given for the squire's attempt to kill Gawayne
either at the inception of his action or when his guilt is re
vealed. His anonymity and the motivelessness of his crime sho
his lack of importance as a human being, but instead indicate hi
function as the agent of the evil that has begun to manifes
itself in the court. He, as did the serpent in Eden, presents
woman with an apple and lets nature take its course. The intro
duction of the apple at this point makes the connection betwee
Eden and Camelot quite evident, as if it were a deliberate remir
der that this is a retelling of the biblical story. And here too
the results of the action determine the future. Gaynor, as di
Eve before her, becomes the means by which discord and deat
arise. The knight to whom the queen offers the apple, and wh
dies of its poison, is by virtue of his resemblance to Lancelot
being both foreign and dear to Gaynor, a reasonable proxy fo
Lancelot in his role of Adam. Gaynor's offering of the apple t
him, innocent in itself, could be attributed to fate. But her
fate is less the result of coincidence than the result of some
thing evil determined to turn events to its own use. The juxtapc
sition of Gaynor and the apple also, of course, indicates he
connection with "forbidden fruit" and is a reminder that it i
Lancelot and Gaynor's unlawful desire for each other that has bee
the initial cause of this second Fall.

This manifestation of evil is followed by others. Mordre
becomes free to work his mischief as another agent of that malevo
lence. He is, however, far more of a threat than the nameles
squire, for he is the epitome of the evil that hovers over th
court. Appearing only when the chance of causing dissensio

vails itself, he is first seen with his brothers, anxious to let
the king know of Lancelot and Gaynor's adultery, and quick to be
the of the party of knights that attempt to trap the lovers in the
queen's chamber. As the evil in the court grows, Mordred correspondingly takes on more importance until he becomes the personification of this force, grown so strong that it threatens to usurp
all rightful authority and morality. Mordred's attempts to take
his father's kingdom and his father's wife are the signs of the
inroads that evil has made in Arthur's court. Although Arthur
does finally slay Mordred, proving that the power of God is
greater than that of evil, the death wound that Arthur receives
from Mordred attests to the power that evil has to destroy man,
for not even the death of Mordred can undo the damage already
done.

Arthur's dreams before the last battle have been a warning of
what is to come, and although in his second dream the ghost of
Gawayne advises him how to avert the disaster foretold in the
first dream, the growth of evil has moved events too inevitably to
the point where the catastrophic battle must take place. And it
is here that it is the serpent, so strongly reminiscent of Genesis, that is the means of ensuring the downfall of what was once
good and beautiful. Nowhere throughout the poem is the force of
evil shown more clearly in its true form, for here at the ultimate
moment, it reveals itself in its primordial guise. For this,
surely, is the same serpent that led to man's first Fall. Having
patiently waited for man to repeat the mistakes he made in Eden
and nurtured by the chaos resulting from man's misuse of free-will, evil appears in tangible form to make certain that nothing,
not even man's most rational and earnest attempts to contravene
the outcome of his actions, will prevent the destruction its
nature seeks.

In this climactic episode of the story, that which appears to
be the result of uncontrollable, blind fate, is, nonetheless, the
fault of man. It is man's actions that have led to the two armies
confronting each other; it has been man alone who had made the
choices leading to this unfortunate state; and it is man alone who
is responsible for the outcome. The adder may seem to be the
cause of the battle, but it was man's actions that gave evil the
power to bring about this death and destruction.

The finality of this loss of a second Eden is illustrated by
the hand that emerges from the depths of the sea to receive Arthur's gleaming sword, which it brandishes, and with which it
disappears beneath the surface of the water.

> There cam an hand, wyth-outen reste,
> Oute of the water, and feyre it hente,

> And brandysshyd as it shuld brast,
> And sythe, as gleme, a-way it glente. (SM 3490-3493)

In Genesis, God places a flashing, whirling sword in the hands of the guardians He stations at the boundaries of Eden to prevent man from ever returning there. The reception of Arthur's sword by the mysterious hand is, similarly, the sign that man is again barred from an earthly paradise. Having been given a second chance to have an Eden on earth, man has again lost it through his own actions.

Man, the <u>Morte</u> seems to say, will never have an Eden in the temporal world. Given his nature, the power of free-will, that mixed blessing, will forever doom him to make the decisions that lead to his fall. Only when he can give up the promptings and the desires of his earthly nature, will he find paradise. Both Gaynor and Lancelot, who had chosen freely to satisfy their own desires rather than God's will, become at the end of the tale, the examples of the way in which this paradise may be found. By renouncing their love and retiring from the pleasures of the world into lives of prayer and repentance, they show their wish to atone for their sins. That this atonement is pleasing to God is indicated by the bishop's dream on the night of Lancelot's death.

> here was launcelot bryght of blee,
> wyth angellis xxx thousand and sevyn;
> him they bare vp on hye,
> A-gaynste hym openyd the gatys of hevyn. (SM 3876-3879)

Man will never again find his paradise on earth, but through the Fall he has acquired the knowledge of good and evil. Having the ability to distinguish between the two, he must take the responsibility for the choices he makes. While his nature has made it certain that man will never again find Eden in this world, his earnest attempts to obey God, and his sincere repentance for his sins may bring him to the paradise found in salvation when his earthly life is over. For while he lives, despite his intensions, man is weak, and his weakness will forever doom him to repeat the story of the First Fall.

This message found in the Stanzaic <u>Morte</u> would not have seemed to a medieval audience to be inconsistent with the romance and adventure found in the tale, nor would these have, in any way, obscured the message. In fact, the moral may well have contributed to its popularity with an audience that might have expected that even a poem meant primarily as an entertainment would contain within itself a consideration of man's relationship to God.

The Translation

The written English of the late middle ages was not too much different from that of today, and much of the Stanzaic Morte can probably be understood by a modern reader without too much difficulty; however, many words and phrases that are obsolete, inconsistent in spelling and unfamiliar in usage do present the reader unversed in Middle English with some problems that can interfere with the appreciation and enjoyment of the work.

Larry D. Benson's edition of King Arthur's Death provides a version of Le Morte Arthur in which the spelling has been regularized and his edition provides, as well, a useful page by page glossary that makes the reading of the poem somewhat less complicated than earlier editions, and to which I am indebted for some of my translation.

The stanzaic Morte has never, to my knowledge, been translated completely into Modern English in its original verse form. Because of its position in the history of Arthurian literature, and because it is an interesting and charming version of a tale important to the Arthurian cycle, it deserves a wider audience. For this reason I have attempted a verse translation of the poem.

I have kept as closely as possible to the original, maintaining the sequence and the rhyme scheme of the stanzas, using whenever possible the wording of the original, using when necessary, the medieval device of rhyming a word with itself; and, as in the original, there are places where the rhyming is not exact. I have kept most of the romance cliches wherever they appear, to retain the feeling of the minstrel style of the original.

I have taken one liberty, however, with the poem. I have added the two stanzas that follow stanza 148 and the first two lines of stanza 149 to carry the action of the narrative over the gap caused by the missing page of the original manuscript.

The Story of Le Morte Arthur

King Arthur, concerned that his Round Table is on the decline, holds a tournament which will bring the knights back to court by giving them the opportunity to demonstrate their prowess and win honor and fame. This, he hopes, will restore the court to the state of perfection it held before the knights left to search for the Holy Grail.

The tournament is to be held in the city of Winchester, and the knights come from all parts of the world, each determined to

show himself as the best. Among these knights is Lancelot d
Lake, long the lover of Arthur's queen Gaynor.

On the first day of the tournament, Arthur and most of hi
knights leave for Winchester. Lancelot remains behind as doe
Agravayne, the king's nephew, who is suspicious of the queen an
Lancelot and hopes to catch them "in the act." He is disappointe
this day, however, as Lancelot, apparently suffering some qualms
takes leave of the queen to go to Winchester. Gaynor is anxiou
for him to go, as she is aware of Agravayne's interest in thei
actions.

Not wanting to be recognized, Lancelot appears in Winchester
in the guise of an old feeble knight. Arthur and Sir Ewain recog
nize him, but say nothing so that he may reveal his identity whe
he wants to. Lancelot, his identity unrevealed, is welcomed t
spend the night at the nearby castle of the Earl of Ascolat wh
dwells there with his two newly knighted sons and his daughter
One of the young knights having fallen ill, the earl and Lancelo
agree that Lancelot will accompany the other to the tournamen
wearing his brother's red arms. During Lancelot's brief stay a
Ascolat, the earl's beautiful young daughter falls in love wit
him. Although he tells her that he loves someone else, he agree
to wear her sleeve in the tournament.

In the morning, Lancelot and the young knight leave fo
Winchester, both bearing red arms. After deciding that they wil
support the weaker party, that which opposes the king's, the
spend the night at the castle of the younger man's aunt and ente
the tournament the following day.

Ewain, Bors, and Lionel ride against Lancelot, not knowin
who he is, and are unhorsed and defeated, but not before inflic
ting a serious injury on Lancelot that causes him to leave th
field and return to the castle of his companion's aunt who send
for leeches to treat his wound.

As Lancelot lies badly injured, the king, curious about th
unknown knight who has defeated some of his strongest knights
decides to lure him back by calling another tournament. One o
the heralds sent to carry the announcement of the tournamen
throughout the country stops at the castle where Lancelot lie
In his determination to attend the tournament, Lancelot attempt
prematurely to arise from his bed, but his exertions cause hi
wound to reopen and he is forced to remain where he is.

The herald, returning to the king, recounts this story t
him, unaware that the knight of whom he has spoken is Sir Lance
lot, but the king realizing that this is the mysterious knigh
that he is seeking, and that he is not well enough to fight, call

off the new tournament and returns to Camelot, expecting to find
Lancelot there. When he does not, Bors, Lionel and Ector set off
to search for Lancelot. They find him at Ascolat where the earl
has taken him to recuperate from his wound. Lancelot tells them
that he was the mysterious knight who had defeated them, and they
forgive each other lovingly for the injuries sustained during the
tournament. The three knights then leave for court to report that
they have found Lancelot. They bear, as well, a message from him
to the queen telling her not to long for him as he will shortly be
returning to her. Once the king and court know of Lancelot's
whereabouts, they eagerly await his return, except for Gawayne who
is so impatient to see him that he promptly leaves for Ascolat to
see him there.

Lancelot, now fully recovered, rides out from Ascolat leaving
his armor behind at the request of the earl's daughter for something of his to comfort her while he is gone. This she shows to
Gawayne when he arrives, telling him that she is Lancelot's sweetheart. Gawayne, recognizing the armor as Lancelot's, returns to
court where he tells Arthur and Gaynor that Lancelot is in love
with the maid of Ascolat. The heartbroken queen confronts Lancelot on his return and he, in ignorance of Gawayne's story, interprets the queen's hysterical anger and recriminations as an expression of her desire never to see him again. He leaves court,
therefore, to the sorrow of Arthur and that of his knights who
blame Gaynor for his going.

Not long after Lancelot's departure, Gaynor is accused of the
murder of a Scottish knight to whom she gave an apple poisoned by
a squire who had intended the fruit for Gawayne. When the
knight's brother Sir Mador hears of this, he demands, as his
right, the death of the queen. It is agreed that the queen must
find a champion to defend her in combat with Sir Mador or must
submit to death.

As Arthur and Gawayne discuss this situation, they see a boat
drifting down the river that flows through Camelot, and in it the
two find the maid of Ascolat, dead and bearing a letter in which
she attributes her death to Lancelot's refusal of her love. When
the queen finds that Lancelot was not in love with the maid, she
regrets her misjudgment of him, but her treatment of Lancelot has
resulted in much resentment toward her by the knights, and she is
unable to find one to defend her against Mador's accusations. In
her fear, she humbles herself before Bors, Gawayne, Lionel and
Ector and begs for their help. They refuse her, angered that she
is the cause of Lancelot's leaving court forever. Bors is finally
moved by his pity for her and agrees to defend her, but Lancelot,
who in his wanderings had heard of Gaynor's troubles, arrives in
time to take Bors' place in battle against Mador whom he defeats.

The guilty squire is apprehended and executed and Mador gladl reconciles his quarrel with Gaynor.

Agravayne, who has long suspected Lancelot and Gaynor o adultery, tells his brothers that it is their duty to report thi treachery to Arthur, their uncle. Gawayne cautions him agains this and he, Gaheris and Gaheriet refuse to take part in wha Gawayne feels will lead to disaster. Agravayne, nonetheless tells Arthur, and they set a trap to catch Lancelot and Gayno together. The unsuspecting Lancelot is found in the queen' chamber by Agravayne, Mordred, and their knights. Lancelot, i his attempt to escape death, slays all the knights including Agra vayne; only Mordred escapes to bring word to the king. Lancelo summons all his men and they leave Camelot. The queen is sen tenced to be burned, but Lancelot and his knights battle throug the men guarding her and rescue her and take her to Lancelot' stronghold, Joyous Gard.

Among those killed by Lancelot in the battle to rescue th queen are Gawayne's brothers, Gaheris and Gaheriet. Gawayne, no having lost three brothers to Lancelot, vows that he will not res until he has killed him. Arthur assembles a mighty host and lay siege to Joyous Gard. In the ensuing battle, Lancelot courteousl refuses to fight with either Arthur or Gawayne, and even mount the king on his own horse after Arthur's is slain. After man casualties suffered on both sides, Lancelot's party wins th battle and the king's forces withdraw.

News of this state of affairs in England reaches Rome, an the Pope sends notice to Arthur that he must make peace wit Lancelot and that he must take back the queen or all of Englan will be placed under interdict. Arthur agrees and when the Pope' message reaches Lancelot, he too agrees to obey the Pope. Lance lot himself returns the queen to Arthur, swearing that Gaynor' honor is unstained and seeking a reconciliation with Arthur. Th hatred that Gawayne has for Lancelot precludes this, and Arthu can only guarantee Lancelot and his men safe passage out o England to their homeland of Benwick, warning him that he wil soon follow to continue the war.

After Lancelot's departure, Arthur prepares to follow leaving Mordred, his nephew and illegitimate son, as steward o England. When Arthur and his men arrive in Benwick from over th sea, they begin to burn and destroy all before them. Lancelot with compassion for his suffering people, sends a message t Arthur requesting a truce to discuss making peace. To this Arthur and most of his men would like to agree, but Gawayne implacable in his hatred for Lancelot, will not release the kin from the vow he has made to revenge his nephews' deaths. Lance lot's castle is soon besieged by Arthur's forces, and Gawayn

xvi

offers a challenge to all knights for single combat. Bors and Lionel are the first and second to respond, and both are defeated. For more than half a year, Gawayne repeats his challenge, wounding or killing every opponent and remaining himself unhurt. Finally, he challenges Lancelot, calling him a traitor and a murderer. Lancelot's honor will not let him disregard this, despite his disinclination to harm one of the blood of King Arthur, and he and Gawayne meet to battle. Although Gawayne is protected by a spell which causes his strength to grow exceedingly from morn until noon, Lancelot withstands his blows until noon and then strikes Gawayne so severely upon the head that he nearly takes his life. Upon recovery from his wound, Gawayne again challenges Lancelot, and again he is defeated by Lancelot who strikes him powerfully upon his old wound. when he finally recovers and is prepared to fight with Lancelot once again, word comes from England that Mordred, who has circulated false reports of Arthur's death, has been crowned king of England and plans to make Gaynor his wife. Arthur and his men immediately take ship to return to England.

In order to save herself from Mordred, Gaynor barricades herself in the Tower of London where Mordred, despite his efforts to breach the walls, is unable to gain entrance. The Archbishop of Canterbury tries to dissuade him from committing the incestuous act of marrying his father's wife and excommunicates him when he refuses to obey, but the holy man is then forced to flee to the forest in fear of Mordred's rage.

Arthur defeats Mordred's forces lying in wait for him at Dover, and pursues them to Barlam Down where they are confronted by Mordred himself and fresh troops. Mordred's men are again defeated and many are slain on both sides. Among the dead is Gawayne, killed by a blow upon the wound inflicted earlier by Lancelot.

A date to meet for further battle is set by Arthur and Mordred, but the night before the armies are to meet, Arthur is troubled by two dreams. In the first he sits richly crowned and clad on top of the wheel of fortune, looking down in fear at the black, fiend-filled water far below him. Suddenly, the wheel turns, and Arthur falls and is seized by the fiends. Much disturbed by this dream, it is long before he can fall asleep again, and when he does he dreams that he sees Gawayne appear with an angel host to tell him that he must take a month's truce before going to battle, as by then Lancelot and his men will have arrived to help him. If he should fight tomorrow, Gawayne warns him, he will be slain.

The following morning, Arthur sends a message to Mordred requesting a truce. He suggests that peace be made and that Mordred be named as his successor and heir. Mordred agrees to meet with the king to discuss the details of the peace, and it is decided that the two, attended by fourteen knights each, will meet in an open space between, and in view of, the two opposing armies. As they approach the meeting spot, an adder appears and stings one of the knights. Instinctively, he raises his sword to kill it. This action, seen by all, seems to be a hostile action, and battle immediately begins between the two armies. A hundred thousand men perish in the battle and only Arthur, his knights Bedivere and Lucan, and Mordred are left alive. Mordred and Arthur battle, and Mordred is slain, but not before he has dealt Arthur his death wound.

Knowing that he is dying, Arthur commands Bedivere to throw the sword Excalibur into the sea, and after twice attempting to save the sword, Bedivere finally does so. A hand arising from the depths seizes the sword, brandishes it and with it in its grasp sinks back into the water. A ship carrying a group of ladies then appears to take Arthur to Avalon to be cured of his wound.

Left alone, Bedivere wanders through the forest until morning when he comes upon a tomb in a chapel. The hermit living there, once the Archbishop of Canterbury, tells Bedivere that the body in the tomb had been brought during the night by ladies who had buried it and who had left a large sum of money for prayers to be said for the dead man. Bedivere realizes that the body is that of King Arthur and asks to be allowed to stay forever to pray for his king's soul.

Queen Gaynor, upon hearing the tidings of the battle goes to Almsbury where she becomes a nun. Lancelot, unaware as yet of the battle's outcome, has heard of Arthur's trouble and with his knights he sets sail for England to help him. Upon their arrival at Dover, he learns that the king is dead and that the queen has disappeared. He leaves his men in Dover and rides throughout England seeking Gaynor. He eventually reaches a cloister where he recognizes Gaynor who has renounced the world in repentance for her sin with Lancelot, which had led to war and death for so many. Lancelot vows that he too will spend the rest of his life atoning for that sin and rides forth until he reaches the chapel where Arthur is buried. He is welcomed by Sir Bedivere and decides to live out the rest of his life there. He is absolved of his sins by the archbishop and becomes a monk and priest.

Lancelot's men, after waiting a half a year for his return decide to wait no longer. Some return home, but Lionel sets out to find Lancelot. He is killed on his journey, but Bors, who has also sought him, finds him and decides that he too will become a monk at that chapel and remain with Lancelot. Seven more of Lancelot's knights who eventually find their way to him also remain there. For seven years they lead holy lives of prayer and repentance until Lancelot tells them that he is about to die, and requests that they bury him at Joyous Gard. Although they do not believe that Lancelot will die, the archbishop hears his confession and absolves him of his sins. That night the archbishop dreams that he sees Lancelot borne up to heaven by thirty thousand and seven angels, and when the men go to Lancelot they find him dead, and they then prepare to take his body to Joyous Gard.

Lancelot's brother Sir Ector, who has been unsuccessfully seeking Lancelot, finds them at Joyous Gard as they prepare to bury Lancelot, and he too decides to take holy orders and return with them to their chapel. On their return trip they stop at Almsbury where they find that Gaynor too has died, and they take her body with them and bury it alongside that of Arthur's at their chapel which is now known as Glastonbury Abbey.

LE MORTE ARTHUR

1

My lords that are both loved and dear,
Listen to me and I shall tell
Of exploits in a long past year
That to our elders once befell.
In noble Arthur's glorious day
Adventure was a commonplace,
And I shall tell the tales of they
Who lived and died in that short space.

2

The brave knights of the Table Round
Who for the Holy Grail had sought,
Had much adventure thereby found.
This now was done and to end brought.
Their enemies were beat and bound;
Of gold and goods they left them nought.
Four years the knights had now lived sound,
After the deeds that they had wrought

3

Til on a time when it befell,
The king in bed lay by the queen;
Adventures they began to tell
That in their own realm they had seen.
The queen said, "If it please thee well,
Then tell me, Sir, what does it mean
That those who once thy glory did swell,
Now leave to seek a different scene?

4

"Sir, your honor begins to fall.
No longer does the world take heed
Of Lancelot and others, all
Who brave and fearless were in deed."
"Dame," said Arthur, "On you I call
To solve this problem in good speed."
"My lord," said she, "To solve this all,
A tournament is what you need.

5

"Adventures once more would begin
And be spoken of on every side.
Once more could knights much honor win,
And for this honor they would ride.
Let not thy court decline; 'tis sin;
It must live in honor and in pride."
"Dame, thou art right," the king said then,
"No more shall this shame abide."

6

A tournament the king decreed.
At Winchester it was to be.
Galehod came in all good speed;
The best of all that came was he.
But all that came sat proud on steed,
So that the ladies there might see
Who of them was the best indeed,
And who would win most easily.

7

They armed themselves with weapons keen,
And to the field they soon did ride
With shield and helm of brightest sheen
To win great honor and great pride.
But Lancelot stayed with the queen,
Though sick at heart he felt inside.
For the love that was for them between,
He made excuse to there abide.

8

The king sat brave upon his steed,
And forth he went upon his way,
But Agravayne, he felt the need
To stay at home, for truth to say,
There were rumors he did heed
That Lancelot with the queen did lay.
And so to take them in this deed
He watched and waited night and day.

9

Lancelot then forth wended he,
Into the chamber of the queen,
And kneeled him down upon his knee,
And saluted there that lady keen.
"Lancelot, what dost thou here with me?
Though king and all are gone, I ween;
I dread we shall discovered be
Of our love that should not be seen.

10

"Sir Agravayne at home is he,
And night and day he watches us two."
"Nay," he said, "My lady free,
I think not that it shall be so;
I come to take my leave of thee,
And out of court I now will go."
"Yes, and quickly must thou readied be;
Thy staying only brings me woe."

11

Then to his chamber went the knight,
Where rich attire waited there.
He clad himself in armor bright,
So nobly fashioned and so fair,
Took shield and sword he used with might
When in battle he did them bear
And mounted then his horse so light
That the king had given him ere.

12

He held himself not to the highway,
That knight that was hardy and free,
But hastened he both night and day,
Til at last he came to that great city,
Winchester it's called, and truth to say,
Twas there the tournament should be.
King Arthur there in a castle lay
And much there was of game and glee.

13

As men would Lancelot behold
And he would not himself there show,
His shoulders up he then did fold
And down he hung his head full low
As if he couldn't his limbs control,
And heeded not the bugle's blow.
Indeed he seemed as one quite old,
And no man there then did him know.

14

The king stood on a tower high,
Sir Ewayne standing by his side.
"Sir Ewayne," then the king did cry,
"Knowest thou that old knight I just spied?"
Straightwise did Sir Ewayne reply
(What is courteous, one need never hide.)
"Sir, it is but some old knight
Who comes to see the young knights ride."

15

Their eyes stayed on that knight alone,
But mostly for the horse's sake,
And then it stumbled on a stone
Then all its body began to shake;
And each limb of the knight was shown
When up the bridle he did take.
To both it was then quickly known
That the knight was Lancelot du Lake.

16

Then nobly thus, the king spoke he
To Sir Ewayne these words straightwise:
"Well is Lancelot held to be
Of all the world the greatest knight
Of beauty and of bounty;
And there is no one of such might;
At every deed the best is he,
And since he wishes to hide from sight,

17

"Sir Ewayne, we will let him bide.
He thinks that we know him nought."
"Sir, it's best to let him ride
And let him do as he has thought;
He will be here near beside
Since to be here he has sought.
We shall know him by his deed,
And by the horse that he has brought."

18

An earl there was who dwelt nearby,
Lord of Ascolat was called this knight.
Sir Lancelot did thither ride,
And asked if he could spend the night.
They received him with great pride
And with a feast that did delight.
Lancelot, though, his name did hide,
And said he was a foreign knight.

19

Two sons that goodly earl had then,
And newly knighted were the two.
At this time it was the custom of men,
And all young knights did follow true,
That ere their first year of knighthood came to end,
They might bear arms of but one hue,
Red, white, yellow or blue, so then
All men thereby the young knights knew.

20

As they all sat at meat that night,
Lancelot to the earl spoke there:
"Is there here, good sir, some young knight
That to the tournament will fare?"
"I have two sons to my delight,
But one is ill, yet, sir, I swear,
If company I could provide,
My other son, I would were there."

21

"Sir, If your son would go to fight,
With him to Winchester would I ride,
And help him there with all my might
That harm to him would not betide."
"Sir, ye seem a noble knight,
Courteous with noble pride;
At morning breakfast thee aright,
And with my son then shall you ride."

22

"Sir, one thing more I ask thee to do
To which I hope thou will accede.
Hast thou armor, old or new
That I may borrow for this deed?"
"My sick son's armor, sir, should do;
Take his armor, and take his steed;
For my sons then will all take you,
For all in red ye both shall be."

23

The good earl had a daughter dear,
Mighty Lancelot she beheld.
Her face was as bright as a blossom clear
Or a flower that springs in the field.
Glad she was to have him near,
That most noble knight under shield;
Weeping was her greatest cheer,
For the love for him her heart held.

24

Up then rose that quiet maid
And to her chamber she did go,
Where down she fell upon her bed
And nearly her heart burst in two.
Lancelot knew what troubled the maid
By her actions well he knew;
He called her brother, much dismayed,
And to her chamber they did go.

25

He sat him down for the maiden's sake,
Upon her bed where she did lay.
Courteously to her he spake,
For to comfort that fair maid.
In her arms then she did him take,
And these words to him she did say:
"Sir, thee alone can cure my ache,
For save my life no doctor may."

26

"Lady," he said, "thou must not fret,
Nor for me make thyself ill.
In another place is my heart set;
It is not thus at my own will.
On earth is no thing that will not let
Me be thy knight loud or still.
Another time we may be met
When thou may better speak thy fill."

27

"Since I from thee can have no more,
As thou art noble knight and free,
In the tournament then would'st thou bear
Some sign of mine that men would see?"
"Maid, thy sleeve I will gladly wear
And will take it for love of thee.
Never did I for a lady ere,
Save one that had most loved me."

28

On the morrow when it was day
The knights readied themselves with care.
And forth they went upon their way
Together as brothers a pair.
They met a squire by the way
That from the tournament did fare,
And him they asked if he could say
Which party was the strongest there.

29

"Sir Galehod has men the more,
In truth, my lords, as I you tell,
But Arthur is the stronger there;
His knights are those that most excel.
They're bold and fierce as any boar,
Ewayne and Bors and Lionel."
To Lancelot spoke the earl's son there,
"Sir, with them I advise we dwell."

30

Sir Lancelot spoke then indeed,
"As all of these are men of might,
Amongst these how would we succeed,
Where all are strong and stout in fight?
Let up help those who have most need;
Against the best we'll strive, young knight,
And if we there do any deed,
This then will make our honor bright."

31

Lancelot spoke thus at this time
As a knight that was noble and free,
"Tonight, outside I suggest we bide;
The crowd is great in that city."
"Sir, an aunt have I that lives here beside,
A lady of much great beauty.
Were it thy will that there we ride,
To welcome us, she glad would be."

32

Then to the castle did they fare,
Of the lady fair and bright.
Happy was that lady there
That they would dwell with her that night.
Supper for them she did prepare
Of meat and drink, a gladsome sight.
At morn they rose and forth did fare,
Both Lancelot and that young knight.

33

And soon they came into the field
Where much there was of game and play.
And for a while they paused to see
How Arthur's party fared that day.
Galehod's party began to yield,
On foot were his knights led away;
Lancelot stout was under shield
Thinking to help him, if he may.

34

Up to him then rode Sir Ewayne
As fierce and bold as a wild boar.
Lancelot took up his reins,
And in the red armor that he wore
Such a blow he gave with might and main
That Sir Ewayne was unhorsed there.
All men thought he had been slain
So was he wounded wondrous sore.

35

Sir Bors thought it nothing good
When Ewayne from his horse did fall,
And leaped he forth fast as he could
At Lancelot, I tell you all.
Lancelot hit him on the hood,
And he too to the ground did fall;
None so brave e'er had against him stood,
Or against the crowd of one and all.

36

Now Lionel had all this seen,
And so in haste he made him ready.
At Lancelot with heart so keen
He rode with helm and sword so steady.
Lancelot hit him, as I ween,
Right through his helm into his head,
And soon thereafter it was seen
That horse and man went down like lead.

37

Then gathered the knights together there
And crafty counsel did they take;
No such knight could be they did swear,
Save for Lancelot du Lake.
But since the sleeve on his crest was there,
Him for Lancelot they would not take,
For never such would that knight bear,
Unless 'twas for Queen Gaynor's sake.

38

"Of Ascolat he never was,
That so well bears himself today."
Sir Ector then said that in truth,
What this knight was, he would assay.
Then a noble steed did Ector choose,
And forth he rode both glad and gay;
Lancelot he sought, and then in truth,
Between them was no childish play.

39

Ector struck as hard as he could
At Lancelot that very time
Through helm to head with blow so good
That Lancelot near lost all pride.
Then he hit Ector on the hood;
His horse did fall and he besides.
Then Lancelot blinded by his blood
Out of the field full fast did ride.

40

And with the earl's son he did go
Til they came to a forest dark and drear,
And there at last they were alone.
When off his helmet he took there
The young knight cried: "Alas! Oh woe!
This is a mortal wound I fear."
"Nay," the knight said, "That is not so.
But much I wish at rest we were.

41

"Sir, my aunt lives here beside,
Where lately we both spent the night.
Were it thy will there to ride,
She could help us with all her might,
And send for leeches this very time,
Who would your wounds then heal aright.
And I myself shall there abide
And be thy servant and thy knight."

42

Through the forest they took their way
To the lady so kind and fair,
For leeches she called that very day
That lived both far and near.
But by the morn of the next day
So cruel was the pain he did bear
And so sore wounded he did lay,
That oft the thought of death seemed fair.

43

Meanwhile King Arthur with much pride,
Called his knights that were nearby,
And told them a month he would there bide,
And in Winchester would he lie.
Heralds he sent to go and ride,
Another tournament to cry.
"This knight will be somewhere nearby,
For he is wounded bitterly."

44

When the king's letters ready were
The heralds forth with them were sent.
Through all of England they did fare;
The tournament to cry they went.
They told all to hasten and prepare
For that second tournament.
And these letters they did bear
To those of brave and daring bent.

45

Til on a time that it befell
That a herald came by the way
And at the castle a night did dwell,
Where Sir Lancelot wounded lay.
Of the tournament he did tell
That would be that very Sunday.
Lancelot sighed wondrous well,
And said, "Alas and well away!

46

"When knights can win such fame and pride,
That such ill chance keeps me away,
Like a coward here to abide.
This tournament, in truth I say,
For me is made this very time.
Though I should die this very day,
Surely, I shall thither ride."

47

The leech spoke then with voice of doom
And said, "Sir, do you have no thought
Of all the craft that I have done?
All of this will come to nought.
There is no man under the moon,
By Him that all this world has wrought,
Might save your life if that time come
That you upon your steed were brought."

48

"Truly though I die this day,
In my bed I will not lie.
Rather would I do what I may
Than here to die so cowardly!"
The leech then went upon his way;
He would no longer stay thereby.
The knight's wounds burst, then still he lay,
And in his bed he swooned three times.

49

Then sorely wept the lady good,
When she saw that he dead would be,
And the earl's son then in sorry mood,
For the leech again called he,
And said, "You shall have presents good
If you remain and dwell with me."
The leech then staunched Lancelot's blood,
And bade him of good cheer to be.

50

The herald then went on his way
In morning when the day was light,
And swiftly went as ever he may
To Winchester that very night.
He saluted the king, and truth to say,
By him sat Sir Ewayne the knight.
The herald told them of his day,
What he had heard and seen with sight.

51

"Of all that I have seen with sight,
Never was there wonder more
Than when I saw a foolish knight
That in his bed lay wounded sore.
He could not hold his head upright,
Not if all the world he could win there,
But for anguish that he could not ride
All his wounds burst open there."

52

Sir Ewayne nobly then spoke he,
And to Arthur said he there:
"Surely no coward knight is he;
Alas he is not whole and fair.
Full well I know that it is he
That did against us nobly fare.
This tournament is best let be;
In truth, that knight may not come there."

53

The tournament was then no more,
Away the company was sent.
The knights all went their ways to fare,
And each upon his way then went.
To Camelot did Arthur fare,
As the queen there all this time had spent;
He thought Lancelot would be there,
But he found him not to his discontent.

54

For Lancelot sore wounded lay
While knights looked for him far and wide.
The earl's son both night and day
Tended him and never left his side.
When he could ride, the earl that day
Brought him home with noble pride,
And made for him pleasure and play,
Til once more he might walk and ride.

55

Then Bors and Lionel they swore,
As from Arthur they took leave there,
That return they would nevermore
Til they found Lancelot somewhere.
Sir Ector too went with them there
To seek to find his brother dear.
Through many a place the three did fare
As they sought for him far and near.

56

Til on a time that it befell
They came upon that very way
And at the castle did they dwell
There where Lancelot wounded lay.
Lancelot they saw, as I you tell,
Walking along the walls that day.
And on their knees for joy they fell,
Such happy men they were that day.

57

When Lancelot saw those very three
That in the world he loved the best,
A merrier meeting might no man see;
And then he led them to their rest.
The earl himself so glad was he
That he had gotten such a guest.
And so was the maiden fair and free
That all her love on him had cast.

58

When they came to supper that night,
Boards were set and cloths were spread.
The earl's daughter and the knight
Together sat as he them bade.
The earl's sons both then took delight
To serve all, and were far from sad.
The earl himself with all his might
Did all to make them gay and glad.

59

But Bors ever in mind he thought
That Lancelot had been wounded sore.
"Sir, if it is your will to hide it nought,
Then tell us where you so hurt were."
"By Him that all this world has wrought."
Sir Lancelot so boldly swore,
"That blow shall be full dearly bought,
If ever we may meet us more!"

60

Sir Ector truly did not like
The words that he heard there;
For sorrow he lost strength and might,
His countenance lost all its cheer.
Bors then spoke these words aright,
"Ector, I can see quite clear
That it is in truth no coward knight
That you are menaced by here!"

61

Lancelot said, "Ector, you were
He who wounded me so sore?"
Ector spoke with innocent cheer.
"Lord, I knew not who it were;
A blow from you, I too did bear,
And never felt I one so sore."
Sir Lionel by God did swear
His scars would last forevermore.

62

From Sir Bors then these words came.
He was a knight that was wise indeed.
"We all were wounded in that game;
I was thrown from off my steed.
Thy brother, sir, thou must not blame;
But knowing now each other's deed
Remember Ector's might, 'twould be no shame
To seek his aid if you have need."

63

Lancelot laughed with heart so free
That Ector worried so that night.
"Brother, nothing dread thou thee,
For soon I shall be well and right.
Though thou have sorely wounded me,
I'll never blame thee for my plight,
But ever the better love I thee
That such a strong blow thou can smite."

64

The three knights then on the third day
Did take their leave to fare.
To Arthur's court they would away,
But Lancelot remained there.
"Greet well my lord, I do thee pray,
And tell my lady how I fare,
And say I will come when I may,
And tell her not to miss me there."

65

They took their leave, I tell no lie,
And bravely went upon their way.
To the court they did then ride,
There where Queen Gaynor lay.
King Arthur to the forest side
Had gone with knights that very day;
No one was close upon her side;
Their message they could freely say.

66

They kneeled them down before the queen,
These knights so wise of lore,
And said that they had Lancelot seen
And for three days they with him were,
And how that he had wounded been
And sick he had lain full sore.
"Ere long, by thee he shall be seen;
He bade thee long for him no more."

67

The queen then laughed so merrily,
When thus she knew that he was well.
"Oh worthy God, what joy for me,
You now must Arthur quickly tell."
To the forest then rode these knights three,
To the king this good news to tell,
And Jesus Christ then thanked he;
Was never news he liked so well.

68

He called Sir Gawayne to him there,
And said, "Truly, that was he
Who that day did the red arms bear,
And now he lives; O joy is me!"
Gawayne answered with good cheer,
As always courteous and free:
"Never to me was news so dear;
I long for Lancelot to see."

69

Then from the king and from the queen
Sir Gawayne took his leave to ride,
And from the court he then rode out
And quickly on his way he hied
To Ascolat, and there's no doubt
He rode as fast as he could ride,
For til he Lancelot had seen
Neither day nor night would he bide.

70

By then was Lancelot sound and fair
And busied himself to prepare,
For leave he planned to take from there.
The maiden wept with sorrow and care,
"Sir, if that your will it were,
Since I of thee may have no more,
If some thing thou would leave me here
To look on when I miss you sore."

71

Lancelot spoke then courteously
To comfort that lady then,
"My armor shall I leave with thee,
And in thy brother's will I wend;
Lady, thou must not yearn for me,
For more time here I may not spend.
But it shall not a long time be
Ere I shall come or word shall send."

72

Lancelot readied himself to ride,
And on his way he went forthright.
To that castle came Gawayne in time,
And asked he after such a knight.
They greeted him with courteous pride,
A rich supper was prepared that night,
And said, their hearts had nought to hide,
That he was gone for a fortnight.

73

Sir Gawayne did the maiden take
And sat her in his sight,
And spoke of Lancelot du Lake;
That never was other such knight.
The maiden then of Lancelot spake,
Said all her love did on him light,
"For his sweetheart he me did take
And left with me his armor bright."

74

"Now, damesel," he said anon,
"I am full glad that this is so,
For such a lover is that one,
That nowhere in the world I know
Is there a lady of flesh and bone
No matter where in earth thou go,
Even with heart of steel or stone,
Who could from him her love withhold.

75

"But, damesel, I beseech thee
That his shield thou would'st me show.
If Lancelot's indeed it be,
Then by its colors I will know."
The maiden then most courteously
With him to a chamber did go;
Lancelot's shield she let him see,
And all his armor she did show.

76

Sir Gawayne then most courteously
To the maiden there he spake.
"Lady," he said, "It's plain to see
This belongs to Lancelot du Lake.
Damesel," he said, "Much pleased am I
That thee for sweetheart he would take,
And I with all my might will try
To serve as your knight for his sake."

77

Thus Gawayne spoke with words so right,
What his will was for to say
And until he went to bed that night
About him was pleasure and play.
Then took he leave from earl and knight
On the morrow when it was day,
And took he leave from the maiden bright,
And forth he went upon his way.

78

Gawayne knew not which way to ride
Or where Sir Lancelot would be;
Once Lancelot was out of sight,
Most difficult to find was he.
So took Gawayne to the highway wide,
And back to Camelot went he.
Welcomed was he by king and knight
Who greeted him most graciously.

79

Then it befell upon a time
The king stood by the queen and spake,
Gawayne was standing there beside.
While each to each complaint did make
Of how long they did with woe abide
The coming of Lancelot du Lake.
In the court was little pride,
So sorely sighed they for his sake.

80

"Surely if Lancelot was alive,
So long from court he would not be."
Sir Gawayne spoke; I tell no lies:
"No wonder great it seems to me,
For the fairest maid that is alive
Chosen for his sweetheart has he.
No man here but would not sigh
Such a beauty for to see."

81

Then the king much pleased was he
With those tidings he then did hear,
And asked of Gawayne courteously
To tell him what maiden it were.
"The daughter of the earl," said he,
"Of Ascolat as you may hear,
Where I was treated graciously.
His shield the maiden showed me there."

82

The queen then said not one word more,
But quick to her chamber went she,
And down upon her bed fell so,
And wept she there most grievously.
"Alas," she cried, "And well a woe,
That ever life was given me,
For the best man I did ever know
Forever now is gone from me."

83

The ladies that about her stood
And knew what caused her misery,
Bade her to be of comfort good,
And let no man her sorrow see.
Her bed they made with saddened mood
And therein put that sad lady;
Ever she wept, nor stop she could
And much to her ladies' pity.

84

So sorely sick the queen did lay
That sorrow was her only meat,
Til it fell that on one day
Sir Lionel and Ector went
Into the forest, there to play
Where flowers were and branches sweet,
And as they went along their way
With Lancelot then did they meet.

85

With such joy then did their hearts swell
When they their master saw with sight,
That on their knees they quickly fell,
And all then thanked the good God's might.
Such was the joy they knew full well
On meeting with that noble knight.
Then quickly did he bid them tell
How fared his lady bright.

86

Then answered him the two knights free
And said that she was sick full sore.
"Sorrow it is to hear and see
How much she is in grief and care.
And Arthur too so sad is he
In court because you come no more.
Dead he supposes you must be,
As does the court, both less or more.

87

"Were it thy will with us to fare
And speak thee now with the queen,
Happy I know she'd be once more
If once she had again thee seen.
The king is much in grief and care,
And so is all the court I ween.
Dead they have supposed thou were,
So long from court have thou been."

88

Lancelot promised then and there
That home he would now with them ride.
Then made the knights much happy cheer
And hastened them with joyful pride,
And to court did they swiftly fare.
For nothing did they stop or bide
Until Camelot reached they there,
Where all then Lancelot espied.

89

The king stood on a tower on high
And near beside him stood Gawayne
And when Lancelot they spied
Their happiness they showed full plain.
They ran as swiftly as they might,
So glad were they to see him again,
That never seemed a day so bright.
Then kissed him did king, knight and swain.

90

To a chamber the king him led,
And in their arms all did him fold;
They sat him on the richest bed
That was covered with cloth of gold.
To wait on him made no man sad,
But an honor they did it hold
To welcome him and make him glad
While he all his adventures told.

91

Three days in court did he dwell there
And never spoke he with the queen,
So great a crowd was always near
That to see her he had not been.
That lady bright as a flower fair
Sadly she longed most grievously,
Down her face ran many a tear,
And to nobody dared speak she.

92

Then it fell upon a day
The king upon a hunt did ride
Into the forest there to play
With most of his knights by his side.
But Lancelot long in bed he lay,
For that day with the queen he thought to bide.
To her chamber he took his way,
And saluted her with happy pride.

93

First he kissed that lady fair
And saluted her lovingly
And then her ladies with her there,
Whose tears all flowed so happily.
"Woe! Well away!" the queen said there,
"That ever I thee did see!
Alas for the love that we did share,
That it should thus departed be.

94

"Alas, Lancelot du Lake,
Ever thou had my heart in hold,
But now the earl's daughter thou would take,
Of Ascolat, as I've been told!
And now you give up for her sake
All thy deeds of arms so bold;
Woefully may I weep and wake
Til buried I be dead and cold!

95

"But, Lancelot, I beseech thee here
As of necessity this need be so,
That never thee reveal to her
The love that was between us two.
Nor may she be to thee so dear
That deeds of arms thou will not do.
If I may sometimes of thee hear,
Then I can bear my life of woe."

96

Lancelot full still then stood;
His heart was heavy as a stone.
So sorrowful did grow his mood,
He felt his world was overthrown.
"Madame," he said, "For Cross and Rood,
What mean thee by this moan?
By him that wrought me with His Blood,
Of these things you speak know I none.

97

"But by thy words it seems to me,
Away thou would I were.
Now have good day, my lady free,
For thou shalt see me nevermore!"
Out of the chamber then went he,
And his heart was filled with woe.
The lady three times swooned she,
And she almost slew herself there.

98

Lancelot to his chamber went he,
Where all his rich attire lay
And dressed himself most nobly
Though sadness heavy on him lay;
Then forth he sprang like a spark indeed
With sorry face in truth to say;
Then up he mounted on his steed
And to a forest rode away.

99

Tidings came into the hall
That Lancelot was on his steed;
Then came the knights arunning all
To stop him, but did not succeed.
Bors de Gawnes and Lionel
And Ector that was bold of deed,
On horses swift they followed all;
Loud they called but he would not heed.

100

There could no man him overtake;
He rode into a forest green.
Then much moan they began to make,
The knights that were bold and keen;
"Alas," they said, "Lancelot du Lake,
That ever thou did see the queen!"
And her they cursed then for his sake,
That ever love was them between.

101

They knew not ever where to fare,
Nor to what country he would go,
And back they went a-sighing sore,
The knights that were keen and bold.
The queen they found in swooning there
Her comely tresses all unfold,
They were so full of sorrow and care
No comfort for her did they hold.

102

The king then hasted for his sake
And home he came that very day.
He asked for Lancelot du Lake,
And they said, "He is gone away."
The queen was in her bed all naked,
Sore sick in her chamber she lay,
And so much moan the king did make
And no one in the hall did play.

103

The king then called Gawayne that day
And from his lips did his sorrow spill.
"Now is Lancelot gone away;
Return I know he never will."
He said, "Alas and well a way."
And sighed sore and made himself ill.
"That lord we loved has gone away.
In court why will he not dwell?"

104

Sir Gawayne spoke then at this time
And to the king said he there,
"Sir, in this castle shall thou bide;
Comfort thyself and make good cheer,
And all of us shall walk and ride
In all lands far and near;
So secretly he cannot hide
That news of him we will not hear."

105

The knights then sought him far and wide,
But of Lancelot they did not hear,
Til it fell upon a time,
When Gaynor bright as a flower fair
At supper sat upon a time
With Sir Gawayne sitting near;
And sitting at her other side
A Scottish knight that to her was dear.

106

A squire in the court had thought
That very day, if that he might,
With a poison that he had wrought
To slay Gawayne, that noble knight.
In fruit he had it then forth brought
And set before the queen so bright.
A shining apple lay on top,
Its poison hidden from the sight.

107

The squire thought the lady bright
Would to Gawayne offer the best,
But she gave it to the Scottish knight
Because he was a foreign guest.
From it then he took one bite;
For he thought that it was well,
And then he lost both main and might
And quickly died, as I thee tell.

108

None knew what all of this did mean,
But quickly up leaped Sir Gawayne,
And then did all the court, I ween;
And on the table the knight was lain.
"Well away," then said the queen,
"Jesus Christ, what may I say?
Surely now all will believe
That I the Scottish knight have slain!"

109

Medicine was then forth brought;
The queen prayed she in fear,
But all of that did help him nought,
For dead the knight was there.
Such great sorrow the queen then wrought,
That sad it was to see and hear,
"Lord, such misery has me sought,
Will I never be free of care?"

110

No more could they help that knight,
But buried him with honor true,
And candles for him they did light;
In a forest chapel that they knew,
A rich tomb there he had aright,
And a crafty clerk the letters drew
That said there lay the Scottish knight
That Queen Gaynor with poison slew.

111

After this a time befell
That to the court there came a knight,
The slain knight's brother he was, I tell,
And Sir Mador was called this knight.
He was a hardy man and well
In tournaments he liked to fight,
And much in court he loved to dwell,
For a man he was of noble might.

112

Then it fell upon a day
That Sir Mador rode out with pride
Into the forest for to play,
Where flowers were and branches wide.
He found a chapel on his way
As he rode through the forestside;
He knew not that there his brother lay,
But there he thought for mass to bide.

113

A rich tomb there then found the knight
With fair written words that he saw;
A while he stood and read them right;
Then great sorrow to his heart did draw
When he saw the name of the Scottish knight
That Queen Gaynor with poison slew.
And then he lost both main and might
And o'er the tomb he fell in swoon.

114

When from his swoon he did awake
His heart was as heavy as lead;
Sad he sighed for his brother's sake,
And thought he of what to do next.
Then his way to court did he take,
And of nothing stood he in dread;
On the queen complaint did he make
And challenged her for his brother's death.

115

The king full sore then did he dread,
For he might not stand against the right.
The queen with fear was nearly mad,
Though she was guilty not a mite;
For she must either confess the deed
Or find a man for her to fight.
Sore well she knew she'd soon be dead
If she be judged by court of knights.

116

Though Arthur the king of the land was he,
He might not stand against the right,
So he decreed by spear and shield
She must find a man for her to fight,
And if he lose, to death she must yield,
Or judged be by a court of knights.
To this they both their hands upheld
And truly pledged they aright.

117

Then they in certain set a day
For that quarrel to undertake.
The word soon spread through each country
What sorrow that the queen did make.
Then at the last, needless to say,
Word came to Lancelot du Lake;
Where he then sick and wounded lay
Men came to him and of this spake.

118

How that Queen Gaynor the bright
Had cruelly slain with treachery great,
A very noble Scottish knight
With poisoned apple that he ate;
And therefore must that lady find
A knight that gladly for her sake
Would ready be to take her fight,
Else burned she would be at the stake.

119

When that Lancelot du Lake
Had wholly heard of this affair,
With angry sorrow did he shake
Because the queen was in such care;
He swore that vengeance he would take
That day if he living were;
Then he strove his sorrows to slake,
And grew he fierce as any boar.

120

Now leave we Lancelot where he was,
With the hermit in the forest green,
And tell we now more of the case
That touched Arthur the king so keen.
Sir Gawayne that morn to counsel he had
And sorely they mourned for the queen;
Into a tower Gawayne he bade
To talk of what had been.

121

And as they in their talking stood,
Deciding there what best would be,
A river under the tower flowed,
And soon upon it they did see
A little boat of shape full good
Moving towards them in the stream.
None might more fairly sail in flood
Nor better be made from tree.

122

When King Arthur saw that sight
Then greatly wondered he,
For shining was that boat and bright
With cloths as rich as rich could be,
That glimmered like gold in the light;
A gold draped vault they seemed to see.
Then said Gawayne that noble knight,
"Full rich this boat does seem to me."

123

Then said the king, "In truth I know
That such a one I've not seen ere.
Thither I suggest we go;
Some wondrous thing will we see there,
And if within be furnished so
As without, or even more fair,
I dare safely say I know
Adventure will we then find there."

124

Out of the tower down went both
Arthur the King and Sir Gawayne,
And quickly hurried to the boat,
They together, and truth to say
When came they where it then did float
Most carefully at it looked they.
Cloth there was draped over the boat
Which they lifted and then in went the twain.

125

Once inside, I tell thee thus,
Full rich they saw was everything,
And in the middle a fair bed was
Well fit for any Christian king.
Then in truth, ere they could stop
They lifted up its covering.
A dead woman they saw there was
As fair as a blossom in spring.

126

To Sir Gawayne then said the king,
"Truly death was too unfair
That he would do so cruel a thing
To take from the world one so young and fair;
Her loveliness my heart does wring;
Would I knew how came she here,
And who she was this sweet darling,
And from what country she did fare."

127

Sir Gawayne his eyes then on her cast,
And most carefully then looked he,
And well he knew then at the last
That the Maid of Ascolat was she.
Once had he wooed her in the past
And asked her his sweetheart to be,
But she had answered him full fast,
That none but Lancelot's would she be.

128

Then spoke Gawayne, I tell thee true,
"Remember thee not the other day,
When my lady queen and we two
Were together then at play,
And of a maid then I told too
That was loved by Lancelot du Lake?"
"Indeed, Gawayne," the king said true,
"I recall me now what thou did say."

129

"In truth, sir," said the noble knight,
"This is the maid of whom I spake;
And most in the world, no one can hide,
She loved Lancelot du Lake."
"In truth," said the king, "Without a lie,
I rue her death then for his sake.
But why I wonder, did she die;
I think for sorrow death did her take."

130

Then Sir Gawayne, that noble knight,
Searched about the bed of the maid;
A purse found he, rich to the sight,
And of gold and pearls was it made.
Empty it seemed, but was not quite,
For when it in his hand he laid,
On a letter his eye did light,
And much he wondered what it said.

131

What there was written know they would;
Sir Gawayne gave it to the king
And said that open it he should;
Then Arthur broke its silken string,
And found when he did it unfold,
Both the end and the beginning
Was written there, as I was told,
Of that fair maiden's dying.

132

"To King Arthur and all his knights
That belong to the Round Table,
Who courteous are and most of might,
Brave and noble, true and stable,
Admirable in every fight,
And to those in need helpful and able.
The Maid of Ascolat by right
Sends thee greeting without fable.

133

"To all of thee my plaint I make
Of the wrong that on me was wrought;
I do not ask that for my sake
Any of thee should mend it aught.
I only tell it for honor's sake,
For if men through the whole world sought,
No place else would they find thy make;
All honor is here that might be sought.

134

"Therefore, if thou would understand
Why I did for many a day
Love more than any in the land
And why death takes me from the world away,
And if for whom thou would understand
That I did so in longing lay,
The truth I've written by my hand,
For it gains nothing to nothing say.

135

"I tell you now the truth of all,
For whom I have suffered this woe;
This misery have I suffered all
For the noblest knight that may go.
There's none so brave upon the field;
None as royal or fair was so,
But churlish was he in the hall,
Like no one else friend or foe.

136

"Neither foe nor friend, in truth to say,
So discourteous as was this one;
His good manners were all away
And churlish manners he had alone.
No matter how I him did pray,
Kneeling and weeping with rueful moan,
To be my sweetheart, he said ever nay,
And shortly said he would have none.

137

"And then at last, lords, for his sake,
I took to heart such sorrow and care,
Til then at last death did me take
So that I might needs live no more.
For loving true had I this pain
And was of bliss made bare.
'Twas all for Lancelot du Lake
That all of this pain did I bear."

138

When Arthur that most noble king
Had read the letter and seen the name,
He said to Gawayne without lying,
That Lancelot was much to blame
And that he deserved reproving
Forever, and much wicked fame.
"Since she died for her great loving,
That he refused her may bring him shame."

139

To the king then said Gawayne,
"I lied about him when I said
That he belonged, as I did say
To a lady or some young maid.
Truth thou said then and it is plain
That he his love would never lay
In so low a place and vain,
But would love a highborn lady gay."

140

"Sir Gawayne," the king said true,
"Now your best advice I need.
What can we for this maiden do?"
Sir Gawayne said, "So God me speed,
If thou will assent thereto,
We shall her with honor lead
Into the palace and bury her so
As befits a duke's daughter indeed."

141

To that the king assented soon;
Gawayne ordered that men come there
And honorably as should be done
To the palace her they did bear.
And then Arthur the king made known
To all his barons, less and more,
How Lancelot would not grant her boon,
And so she died for grief and care.

142

Then to the queen went Sir Gawayne,
And began to tell her of the case:
"In truth, madame," to her he said,
"I yield me guilty of trespass;
About Lancelot I did feign
When I told thee in this place,
That all of his love given plain
To the duke's daughter of Ascolat was.

143

"Of Ascolat, that maiden free
I said his love had won;
That I so lied, it now grieves me,
And truth I tell thee as I can;
That he loved her not, we now well see
And for this died she as white as swan.
This letter here the proof will be;
Her plaint she makes to every man."

144

The queen with anger was near blind,
And to Gawayne said she then:
"In truth, sir, thou were too unkind
To speak that way of any man,
Unless thou knew within thy mind
Whether it was truth or none.
Thy courtesy was all behind
When thou that story first began.

145

"Thy honor now is hurt greatly;
Such a wrong to do that noble knight,
When never did he injure thee.
Why should thou without the right
Lie of him so villainously
Behind his back and out of sight,
When never could thee know wisely
What harm had come and what yet might?

146

"I once did think thee brave and true
And full of noble courtesy,
But I like not thy manners new;
They have all turned to villainy;
Thy brother knights mischief thou do
To lie about them for envy.
Who honors thee, that may them rue;
Therefore, depart my company!"

147

Gawayne then wisely went away;
He saw she was aggrieved sore.
No more to her then would he say,
He would not face her anger more.
The queen then as if she crazy were
Wrung her hands and cried: "Well away!
Alas that ever I was born
For so wretched am I this day!

148

"Heart, alas, however thou could
Believe that Lancelot du Lake
Were so false and fickle of mood
That other love than thee he'd take;
Nay truly for the whole world's goods
No such pain for me would he make."

* * *

The maiden who was fair and free
The duke's daughter of Ascolat,
With honor now was buried she
In the chapel of Camelot;
And on her tomb where men could see
These words were skillfully wrought:
"Now in this chapel here lies she
Who died for love of Lancelot." *

* * *

Meanwhile there passed both day and night
And the king much sadness had he,
For in his court there was no knight
That would battle do for the queen;
The queen was almost mad with fright
And lamented piteously:
"Alas, that none for me will fight
And to shameful death must I go," said she.*

149

[On the day Mador would have his right
Still sought the queen, that sorry dame]*
To find a man for her to fight,
Or she must yield her to the flame.
If judged she were by a court of knights
Her death would be one of shame;
Though innocent she was aright,
There was no knight believed her claim.

150

Much sighed the king and made himself ill
And to Sir Gawayne then went he
And to Sir Bors and Lionel
And to Ector that brave was in deed,
And asked if any were in will
To help him in his mighty need;
The queen on knees before them fell,
Near out of her wits was she.

*I have written these two stanzas and the first two lines stanza 149 to carry the narrative over the gap at this point the original manuscript.

151

The knights answered with little pride,
Their hearts were full of sorrow and woe;
They said: "We saw and sat beside
The knight that she with poison slew,
And that in truth we cannot hide;
Gawayne him onto the table drew.
Against the right we will not ride;
In truth saw we what happened so."

152

Then wept the queen and sighed full sore,
But to Bors de Gawnes went she though;
On knees before him fell she there,
It seemed her heart would burst in two.
"O pity me!" she said, "Lord Bors,
Today to my death shall I go
Unless thy worthy will it were
To save my life and end my woe."

153

Sir Bors de Gawnes so still he stood,
And away his eyes in anger went:
"Madame," he said, "By Cross on Rood,
Full well thou deserve to be burnt;
The noblest body of flesh and blood
Whose life on earth was ever spent,
For thy will and thy wicked mood
From out of our company went."

154

Then she wept and made herself ill
And to Sir Gawayne then went she,
And on her knees before him fell;
Out of her wits she seemed to be.
"Mercy!" she cried there loud and shrill:
"As no guilt have I of this deed,
Would it be thy worthy will
Today to help me in my need?"

155

Sir Gawayne answered without pride;
His heart was full of sorrow and rue:
"Dame, saw I not and sat beside
The knight that thou with poison slew,
And the truth I cannot hide
That I onto the table him drew.
Against the right I will not ride;
The deed I saw thee do."

156

Then went she to Lionel,
That ever had been her own knight;
On her knees before him she fell,
And almost lost she main and might:
"Mercy!" she cried there loud and shrill:
"Lord, as guiltless I am quite,
Would it be thy worthy will
For my life to take this fight?"

157

"How can thee to us thy pleading take,
When thou knows more than any
That thou have Lancelot du Lake
Taken out of our company?
And now much moaning do we make
And in sorrow we do sigh;
By Him that did the first man shape,
We will be glad to see thee die!"

158

Then full sore the queen did dread
And for her life feared she,
And loud she grieved and long she wept,
And before Sir Ector fell on knee:
"For Him that on the Cross was spread
When the crown of thorns wore He,
Sir Ector help me in my need
Or today I die!" said she.

159

"How can thee to us thy pleading take;
Or think that I for thee would fight
That sent away Lancelot du Lake,
That ever was thine own true knight?
My dear brother for your sake
I never more shall see with sight.
Cursed be he that the battle take
To save thy life against the right!"

160

No man there would the battle take;
The queen to her chamber did go,
And such sad moan did she there make
That her heart nearly burst in two.
In sorrow did she shiver and quake,
And she said: "Alas and well a woe!
Why have I not Lancelot du Lake,
Who to battle for me would go.

161

"Evil do I count the deed,
That I have honored many a knight
[But no man have I in my need]*
That for love of me dare take the fight.
Lord, King of all the world indeed,
That do all men rule by right,
Care for Lancelot I plead,
Since he no more will I see with sight."

162

The queen she wept and made herself ill
For she knew that the fire was near
And full sorely mourned she still,
And again to Bors went she there,
And pleaded that it be his will
To help her in her sorry care.
Into a swoon before him she fell
And words could she speak no more.

*A line is missing here in the original manuscript. I have used F.J. Furnivall's suggested line "And I haue no man in my nede." as mentioned in the Rhys edition of the poem as the basis of the above.

163

When Bors the queen saw in such fright
For her he had great pity
And held her in his arms upright
And bade her of good comfort be:
"Madame, unless there come a better knight,
That would the battle take for thee,
I myself for thee shall fight
While any life may last in me."

164

So wondrous happy was the queen
That Bors de Gawnes for her would fight
That nearly in her joy swooned she
Had not Sir Bors held her upright.
To her chamber the queen led he
To her maidens and ladies bright,
And told her that this should secret be
Til he was armed for the fight.

165

Sir Bors that was so bold and keen
Called he then all the other knights
To tell them what he now had done,
And told them as best he might
How he had promised to the queen
That very day for her to fight;
His duty now was plainly seen;
He would save her life if he might.

166

The knights with sorrow to him spake,
And said to him with certainty:
"She has Sir Lancelot du Lake
Caused to leave our company;
No man this battle would not take
Before she did such villainy
But we will not so glad her make
Before we let her be sorry."

167

Bors and Lionel the knight
And Ector that brave was of deed,
They to the forest went aright
To pray at the chapel in their need
To ask the Lord God full of might
That he would give to Bors goodspeed
And grace of God to win the fight,
For Mador they dreaded indeed.

168

As they came to the forest side,
Their prayers at the chapel to make,
The noblest knight then saw they ride
That ever did heaven shape;
All about him gleamed with pride
Black was his steed, his armor and cape;
His name from thee I will not hide,
It was Lancelot du Lake.

169

No wonder were they happy men
When they their master saw with sight,
And on their knees they all fell then
And gave thanks to God All-mighty;
No greater joy had ever been
Than their meeting with this noble knight;
And shortly after asked he then:
"And now how fares my lady bright?"

170

Bors then told him what he might
There was nothing that he did hide,
How there had died a Scottish knight
While a-sitting at the queen's side:
"Today, sir, is her death in sight,
And so no longer may I bide
As for her I have taken the fight.

171

"Although Sir Mador strong may be,
Today he must well prove his might."
"To the court now go ye three
And comfort there my lady bright,
But look thee speak no word of me;
I shall come as a foreign knight."

172

Sir Lancelot that was much of might
Abided in the forest green;
To the court went the other knights
For to comfort the queen.
To make her glad with all their might,
Much good cheer did they let be seen
So that no dread would her affright,
And of good comfort they bade her be.

173

The boards were set and cloths were spread;
The king himself had gone to sit
When the queen was to the table led
With cheeks that were so wan and wet;
So sorrowful they were and sad,
That neither one could eat a bit;
The queen of death was so in dread
That as she sat she grimly wept.

174

And as they came to the third course,
The king and queen and every knight,
Then came Sir Mador on his horse
With helm and shield and hauberk bright
Among them all before the dais;
Upon the queen then cried that knight
To have the right of his cause
As their covenant said he might.

175

The king he looked at every knight,
Never before had he such woe,
For on no one did his eye alight
That against Sir Mador would go.
Sir Mador swore he by God's might,
For he was a man fierce and bold,
That if he were to have his right
He would deal the queen's death blow.

176

Then spoke King Arthur of much might
That courteous was to all men,
"Sir, sit and eat, tis not yet night;
This day has not yet come to end;
Yet might there still come some brave knight
If it God's will were him to send
To give to thee thy fill of fight
Ere the sun to the ground does wend."

177

Bors then laughed at Lionel
For none knew of their secret words;
He went to the chamber where he did dwell
Without saying another word
And armed he himself at his will
With helm and hauberk, spear and sword;
Again he came into the hall
And set him down to the board.

178

The tears ran onto Arthur's knee
For joy when he saw that sight;
And then happily up rose he
And Bors enfolded in embrace tight
And said: "Sir Bors, may God bless thee.
That in this great need thou would fight;
Well for it do you repay me
That I ever honored any knight."

179

Then as Sir Mador loudly spake,
And for vengeance on the queen did call,
Came Sir Lancelot du Lake
Riding straight into the hall'
His steed and armor were all black,
His visor he had let fall;
Many a man began to quake,
So afraid of him were they all.

180

Then spoke Arthur, great of might,
As ever courteous was he:
"Sir, is it your will to alight
To eat and drink with this company?"
Sir Lancelot spoke as a foreign knight:
"Nay, sir." He said most courteously,
"I heard I would here find a fight;
I come to save a lady's life!" said he.

181

"All wasted are the queen's good deeds,
And she has honored many a knight,
If she has no man in her need
That for her life dare take a fight.
Thou who accuse her of misdeed,
Be thou prepared aright,
Though like one mad thou fight on steed,
Today shall thou need all thy might!"

181

Sir Mador was as happy there
As fowl of day after the night,
And to his steed went without care,
As a man who was much of might.
Then to the field they both did fare,
Followed by all, king and knight;
The battle they would see and hear,
And never saw they stronger fight.

183

Soon unhorsed had both knights been
When they met with might and main,
But on they fought with swords so keen,
Both on foot, and truth to say,
Of all the battles that Lancelot had seen
With fierce attacks of might and main,
Never before had he thus been
So in danger of being slain.

184

There was so wondrous strong a fight,
No weakness each in the other found;
From early noon til late at night
Each gave many a woeful wound;
Lancelot then struck with might
And Mador fell at last to ground.
"Mercy," cried that noble knight,
For he was sick and sore unsound.

185

Though Lancelot was fierce as a boar
He stopped then and sternly did stand;
No blow then would he strike more,
His sword he threw from out his hand;
Sir Mador then by God he swore:
"I have fought in many a land
With knights both less and more,
And never have I my match found.

186

"But, sir, a prayer I do now make
By all in life that best loves thou,
And for Our Most Sweet Lady's sake,
That thy name thou would let me know."
Then Lancelot up his visor did take,
And his face then did he show.
When he saw Lancelot du Lake
Was never a man happy so.

187

"Lord," said he, "'Tis well for me
That boast I now may make
That I have stood one blow of thee
And fought with Lancelot du Lake;
My brother's death forgiven be
To the queen, my lord, for thy sake."
Lancelot kissed him with heart so free
And in his arms did him take.

188

Arthur the king then loudly spake
Among his knights to the queen:
"Yonder is Lancelot du Lake,
If him ever with sight I have seen."
To the field then ran they for his sake,
The king and all his knights keen;
Into their arms they did him take;
No gladder men had ever been.

189

Then so happy was the queen
When she saw Lancelot du Lake,
That in her joy near fainted she
But that up the lords did her take.
Then wept and laughed the knights so free
For joy as they together spake
With Sir Mador, and soon with he
They did a new accordance make.

190

No longer did they there abide
But to the castle rode they
With trumpeters and with great pride,
Such joy it was for all that day,
Though Sir Mador might not walk nor ride,
To the castle carried him they,
With brave knights riding at each side
To make him both happy and gay.

191

The squires then were taken all
And tortured with much pain
To find who had served in the hall
When the knight was with poison slain.
Then one was found among them all
Who did the truth speak plain,
How in an apple he put the gall
That he had meant for Sir Gawayne.

192

When Sir Mador heard all the right
That guiltless had the lady been,
For sorrow lost he main and might
And on knees fell before the queen.
Lancelot lifted him upright
For the love that was between;
And kissed he then both king and knight
And happy did all seem.

193

The truth about the squire learned,
Then as was both the law and right,
Drawn and hanged he was and burned
Before Sir Mador that noble knight.
Then to the castle Joyous Gard they turned
And there remained with great delight,
And Lancelot who praise had earned,
Was honored there with all their might.

194

A time befell, the truth to say,
The knights stood in chamber and spake;
Both Gaheriet and Sir Gawayne
And Mordred who could much mischief make.
"Alas," then said Sir Agravayne,
"We false men of ourselves do make.
How much longer shall we sustain
The treason of Lancelot du Lake?

195

"Without a doubt, full well know we
That Arthur our uncle is he,
And if Lancelot lies with the queen,
Against the king traitor is he;
All the court knows what has been
And every day all hear and see.
We should tell Arthur of the queen;
Take thee this counsel of me."

196

"Well know we," said Sir Gawayne,
"That we are to the king his kin,
But Lancelot has such might and main
That such words were better kept in.
Well know thou brother Agravayne,
That only harm by them we'd win;
Better that we should silent remain
Than for trouble and war to begin.

197

"Well know thou brother Agravayne,
None fiercer than Lancelot does go;
And king and court had oft been slain
Had he not been so fierce and true;
And also," then said Sir Gawayne,
"For love that is between us two,
Lancelot will I never betray
Behind his back to his foe.

198

"Lancelot is a king's son good,
And also a hearty knight and bold,
So therefore if in need he stood,
Many a land would with him hold.
And much there would be shed of blood
Because of his tale were it told;
Sir Agravayne, one would be mad
If such an idea he did hold."

199

Then as the knights in this way stood,
Sir Gawayne and the other three,
In came the king in a mild mood;
Gawayne said then: "Brothers, peace!"
The king then said that know he would
Why of their speaking they did cease.
Then Agravayne swore by Cross and Rood:
"Tell thee I shall!" said he.

200

Gawayne to his chamber went,
This tale he would not stay to hear;
Gaheriet and Gaheries in assent
With Gawayne left they there;
Well did they know what all this meant,
And Gawayne then by God did swear;
"Here now is made a commencement
That will not be finished for many a year."

201

Agravayne his feelings did screen
And told the king with words fair and clear
That Lancelot lay by the queen
And so had done full many a year,
And all of this the court had seen,
And each day did they see and hear.
"And we have false and traitors been
That this we have not told thee ere."

202

"Alas," then said King Arthur there,
"In truth that is great pity,
For never a man had ever more
Of beauty or of bounty;
No man ever on earth was there
Who had so great nobility.
Alas, full sorrow if it were
That in him should treachery be.

203

"But if this be so, then without fail,
Sir Agravayne, I plead
That thou will help me with counsel;
How shall we take him with the deed?
Before him do all others quail,
And of him I have much dread;
Nobody would dare him assail
If armed he were upon his steed."

204

"Sir, thou and the court to the forest green
Must go tomorrow for hunting right,
And send word unto the queen
That thou will dwell there all the night,
And I and twelve of my knights keen
Will in secret prepare our might;
We shall take him with the queen
Tomorrow ere the day be bright."

205

At morn with the court to the forest green
The king did a-hunting ride,
And sent he word unto the queen
That there he would all night abide.
And Agravayne with twelve knights keen
At home stayed they that very time,
And all the day they were not seen
For so well did they themselves hide.

206

Then was the queen so wondrous glad
That the king would in the forest dwell,
And quickly Lancelot she bade
To come if that was his will.
But Sir Bors heard these words he had
And to his heart they boded ill;
To Lancelot this good knight said:
"A word, sir, if it be thy will.

207

"Tonight I feel here thou should dwell;
I fear there is treachery nigh,
For Agravayne, I must thee tell,
Watches thee day and night.
Before when with the queen thou did dwell
Never did I worry a mite,
Nor never did my heart feel ill
So much as it does tonight."

208

"Bors," he said, "Now be thee still
And have thou not any more fears;
I shall go to my lady still
Some new tidings for to hear;
I shall do nought but ask her will;
Make thee glad and have no fear,
For certainly I will not dwell,
But come again to thee here."

209

Because he thought to leave there soon,
And to dwell there had he no thought,
None of his armor did he don
But just a robe all richly wrought;
And from his hand his sword hung down;
Of any treachery feared he nought;
There was no man under the moon
That he knew who could harm him aught.

210

When he came to that lady fair
He kissed her and held her tight,
And never had they any fear
That treachery was in sight.
So much of love the two felt there
That leave could not the noble knight;
To bed then with the queen went he
And there he thought to stay all night.

211

Then ere he settled in the bed,
Lancelot in the queen's bower,
Came Agravayne and Sir Mordred
With twelve bold knights strong of power;
Through the door to him they said
That he was false and king's traitor;
Then did Lancelot feel dread,
For he was without his armor.

212

"Well-away," then said the queen:
"What now shall become of us two?
The love that has between us been
To such an ending should it go
Through Agravayne who is so keen
That night and day he's been our foe;
Now it is too clearly seen
That all that was well is turned to woe!"

213

"Lady, thou must stop," he said then,
"All will soon know of this night;
Is there any armor here in
That I may use to save my life?"
"No, in truth," the queen said then.
"Hard will it be to give them fight
Now that armor have I none,
No helm nor hauberk, shield or knife."

214

Ever Agravayne and Sir Mordred
Called him recreant false knight,
And bade him rise out of his bed
For he must of need with them fight;
Then in his robe he did him clad
For no armor he had that night,
He drew his sword and with quick tread
At the chamber door stood he aright.

215

An armored knight did rush there in
And at Lancelot aimed a blow,
So did Lancelot smite him then
That dead to the ground did he go;
The other knights all paused they then
And none the first knight dared follow;
Quick to the door Lancelot went
And locked it against the foe.

216

The knight that Lancelot had slain
Armor had he fair and bright,
For Lancelot this was good gain,
And with it he clad him aright.
"Now know thou well, Sir Agravayne,
Thou imprisons me no more this night!"
Then out he sprang with might and main
Himself against them all to fight.

217

Lancelot fought with steady hand,
Know thee well, I tell thee true!
Sir Agravayne to his death was sent
And so were the other knights too.
None were so strong they could withstand,
Against him nothing could they do;
But Mordred fled like one gone mad,
To save his life was all he knew.

218

Lancelot to his own chamber strode
To Bors and to his other knights;
There Bors armed before him stood;
To bed he had not been that night,
And no sleep had slept those knights so good
Such nightmares did they have that night;
But happy grew they in their mood
When they their master saw with sight.

219

"Sir," said Bors that noble knight,
"About thee we have feared full long;
I dared not go to bed this night
For dread that you had trouble strong.
Our knights so strangely dreamed tonight
That some naked out of bed had sprung,
Because they were in full strong fright
That with thee something was sore wrong."

220

"Sir Bors, dread thee not a mite,
But be of heart strong and bold,
And go and waken all my knights
And see which ones with us will hold;
See they are armed and ready right,
For it is true what thee me told;
We have begun this very night
What will bring many a man full cold."

221

Bors then spoke with dreary mood:
"Sir," he said, "thus shall it be so,
But we shall be of spirit good,
After the well to take the woe."
Up sprang the knights fast as they could
And to ready themselves did they go;
And at morn armed before him stood
A hundred knights and squires too.

222

When they were armed and ready right
At a slow pace forth did they ride
As men that were of much great might
To the nearby forest side.
Lancelot stationed all his knights
And there told them to bide
Til they heard of the lady bright
And what that news should betide.

223

Mordred at home did not remain
But to the forest he did ride
To tell the king, truth to say,
What had happened that very night.
"Mordred, have thou that traitor slain?
Did thou Sir Lancelot smite?"
"Nay, sir, but dead is Agravayne
And so too every other knight."

224

Then these tidings heard Sir Gawayne,
That knight so hardy and bold:
"Alas, then is my brother slain?"
And his heart began to grow cold:
"Warned I well Sir Agravayne,
Ere ever yet this tale was told,
That Lancelot was of so much main
That against him he could not hold."

225

Then no longer would they bide,
The king and all his knights so keen,
But took they council at that time
About what to do with the queen.
And then no longer would they bide;
That day burned to death would she be.

226

The fire made they in the field
And there they brought that lady free,
And all that might a weapon wield
There guarded her most carefully.
But Gawayne who brave was under shield
And Gaheriet and Gaheries would not go to see,
To their chambers they them held,
For her had they such great pity.

227

Then King Arthur at that time
For Gawayne and Gaheries he sent
And their answers I will not hide;
Gawayne to go would not consent,
For he would never be beside
When a woman to death was sent.
But Gaheriet and Gaheries did not bide
And all unarmed thither they went.

228

A squire there all this did see
Who Lancelot to court had sent,
And he to the wood went hastily
Where Lancelot was with his men;
Come they must in haste said he:
"The queen is taken to be burnt!"
Then to horse and arms flew they
And then with great speed off they went.

229

The queen there by the fire stood
In her smock, all ready was she;
Many lords were there strong and good
And great in power were they,
At them came Lancelot fierce as ever he could
And full soon the crowd gave way;
None there was of power so good
To hold him back, so fierce was he.

230

Quickly did they advantage gain,
Attacking with hearts strong and sound;
The lords and knights of might and main
Were fiercely brought to the ground.
Gaheriet and Gaheries both were slain
With many a doleful death wound.
The queen they took, I tell thee plain,
Then to the forest they were bound.

231

The tidings to the king were brought
How Lancelot had taken the queen:
"Such woe as ever man has wrought!
Slain are all our knights so keen!"
Down he fell and swooned he oft;
Such great grief had never been seen;
So near his heart the sorrow sought,
All thought that this his death would mean.

232

"Jesus Christ! What may I say?
On earth was never so much woe;
Such knights as whom today were slain
Are found in all the world no more!
Let no man tell Sir Gawayne
That his brothers to death did go.
O well-away my rueful reign,
That Lancelot should be my foe."

233

Gawayne did still to his chamber hold,
From thence all day he would not go;
A squire to him the tidings told,
And then his heart was filled with woe.
"Alas," he said, "My brothers bold,
Are they then dead? Can that be so?"
And then his heart it turned so cold
That out of life he wished to go.

234

The squire spoke with dreary mood
To try to comfort Sir Gawayne;
"Your brothers know now nought but good
And some day they will come again."
Gawayne ran swiftly as he could
To the chamber where lay the slain;
The chamber floor it ran with blood,
And cloths of gold were on them lain.

235

A cloth he lifted then up high,
What wonder that his heart was sore;
So dolefully to see them lie
That once such noble knights were!
When he his brothers saw with sight
Then words could he speak no more,
And lost he then both main and might
And o'er them fell in swooning there.

236

When from that swoon he did awake,
That hardy knight Sir Gawayne,
By God he swore and loudly spake
As would a man of might and main:
"Between me and Lancelot du Lake
Is no man on earth, truth to say,
Who truce shall set or peace shall make
Til one of us has the other slain!"

237

A squire that Lancelot to court had sent
The tidings did he hear;
Back to the forest then he went
And told he Lancelot there
That king and court did sore lament
For many a man had died there,
And that Gaheriet and Gaheries had also met their end;
This news could Lancelot hardly bear.

238

"Lord," he said, "How can this be?
Jesus Christ, what may I say?
Much love between us there has been.
Alas, that against me they came!
Well know I now that through this deed
A sorry man is Sir Gawayne;
Never will peace between us be seen
Til one of us has the other slain!"

239

Lancelot then with his folk did wend
With sorry heart and dreary mood.
To queens and countesses he did send
And great ladies of gentle blood
For whom he did their lands defend
When they in need of him had stood.
And each her power to him did lend
Which made his party strong and good.

240

Queens and countesses who rich were
Sent him earls of mighty means;
Other ladies that could do no more
Sent him knights or barons free;
So many men to him did fare
That soon a mighty host had he;
To Joyous Gard then went he there
And held him in that strong city.

241

Lancelot's heart was still full sore
For the lady fair and bright;
A damsel he told to prepare;
Richly appareled she would ride
In haste with a message to bear
To Arthur, king of much great might.
To prove the charge false, what might he more
Than offer him therefor to fight?

242

The maiden then prepared to ride
In very rich apparelment
Of green silk cloth that with much pride
Had been wrought in the Orient;
A dwarf went with her at her side
As was Lancelot's commandment.
These were the ways in that past time
When a maid with a message went.

243

Her way to the castle she did make
At the palace she did alight;
To the king her message she spake,
While nearby sat Gawayne the knight.
"Lies have been told of Lancelot du Lake;
True he has been both day and night;
To prove it for his honor's sake
Lancelot offers now to fight."

244

Arthur the king then spoke he there
With words both keen and slow:
"Even if he could prove it nevermore,
Some of my men to death would go;
By Jesus Christ!" the king then swore
As did Gawayne also:
"He for his deeds shall pay full sore,
Unless into him will steel not go!"

245

The maiden then had her answer,
Back to Joyous Gard did she ride
And there what King Arthur's words were
She told Lancelot at that tide.
Lancelot sighed with heart so sore
And tears from his eyes did slide,
And Bors de Gawnes by God then swore:
"With them on battle field we'll bide!"

246

Arthur no longer would abide,
But hasted he with all his might
And ordered messengers to ride
Without a stop both day and night
Through all England on every side
To earl, to baron, and to knight
To bid them come from far and wide
With horses strong and armor bright.

247

For the dead knights there had been much sorrow
And much had there been of care;
So full three hundred men or more
From out their castles tall did fare;
From England and from Ireland also
From Wales and Scotland the best that were
Against Lancelot now would go
With hearts as fierce as any boar.

248

When this host was all arrayed
No longer then did they bide;
Spears were raised and banners displayed
By these brave men who had such pride.
With helm and shield and shining blade
Leading them all Gawayne did ride.
To Joyous Gard their way they made
And there set siege to every side.

249

About the Joyous Gard they lay
For seventeen weeks if not more,
Til it fell upon a day
That Lancelot home bade them fare:
"Break thy siege and go thou away!
To slay thee I could not bear!"
He said: "Alas and well-away,
That ever began this sorrow sore!"

250

Ever the king and Sir Gawayne
Called him false and recreant knight,
They said he had his brothers slain
And traitor he was by day and night;
They bade him come and prove his main
And in the field with them to fight;
Lancelot sighed, for truth to say,
Such sorrow was this to see with sight.

251

Loud to Lancelot did they cry
With voice and harsh trumpeting there;
Sir Bors de Gawnes he stood nearby,
Lancelot's sad face saw he there:
"Sir," he said, "Wherefore and why
Should we these insulting words hear?
Cowardly thou do fare thinks I,
As if thou dared not any man come near.

252

"Dress now we should in rich array
Both with our spears and our shields
As quickly as ever we may,
And ride we then onto the field
And then on this very day,
While life last, my spear I shall wield,
And, sir, to this my life will I lay
That we two will force them all to yield."

253

"Alas," quoth Lancelot, "Woe is me,
That ever I should see with sight
The day that against my lord I be,
That noble king who made me knight!
Sir Gawayne, I beseech of thee,
As a man of great might,
Let not my lord in the battle be,
And thyself with me must not fight."

254

Then no longer could they bide,
And soon the host was arrayed;
When they were ready for to ride
Spears were raised and banners displayed;
And all the host as one did glide
With voices loud and horns that bayed;
Great pity was on either side
That many would lose their lives this day.

255

Sir Lionel with might and main
To give battle was he bound,
Against him then rode Sir Gawayne,
And horse and man he bore to ground,
And all there thought he had been slain;
Sir Lionel had such a wound
That away he was drawn in pain
For he was sick and sore unsound.

256

And on the field through all that tide,
Against Lancelot men fought in vain,
And then as fast as he could ride
He made sure that none would be slain;
The king was ever at his side
Striking at him with all his main,
And he so courteous was all that time
No blow at Arthur would he aim.

257

When Bors de Gawnes this saw at last
Then up to the king he did ride
And on his helm hit him so fast
That the king near lost all his pride;
With broken back his steed down-crashed
And he to the ground fell that time;
And loud words then did Sir Bors cast
At Lancelot him to chide.

258

"Sir, shall thou allow this more
That the king should thee so assail?
With anger in his heart full sore,
Thy courtesy shall not avail;
Battle shall there never be more
If you will let my words prevail.
Give us leave to slay them all," he swore,
"And thus thou will win without fail."

259

"Alas," quoth Lancelot, "Woe is me,
That ever should I see with sight
Before me that unhorsed should be
The noble king who made me knight."
He was so courteous and free
That from his steed he did alight
And the king on it then mounted he
And bade him flee if he might.

260

When the king was mounted there,
Sir Lancelot he looked upon,
Such courtesy this knight had more
Than ever was in any man;
He thought of all that had been ere,
And the tears from his eyes then ran;
He said, "Alas," and sighed full sore:
"That ever yet this war began!"

261

The parties then were drawn away,
Of knights had they both grown thin,
And on the morn of the next day
Again the battle would begin.
They prepared themselves in rich array
And once more both would fight to win.
He that began this wretched play
Had surely committed great sin.

262

Bors was a fierce as any boar
And out he rode to Sir Gawayne,
For Lionel was wounded sore
And revenge for him would Bors gain.
Sir Gawayne did against him fare
As would a man of might and main;
Each through the other's body bore
And both were well near slain.

263

To ground together fell the pair,
On both sides was there woe;
The king's party ready they were
To carry off both of the two.
Then Lancelot himself came near
To rescue Bors he did go;
From each side then men did them bear
So badly wounded were the two.

264

Of this battle much could I tell
To those who would have understood;
How some knights under saddle fell
And down they went with sorry mood,
And steeds that boldly pranced full well
Now waded instead through the blood;
But by the time of the evening bell
Lancelot's party the better stood.

265

And then the battle was no more,
But departed all that day;
Men their friends home led, and bore
Those who slain in the field did lay.
Lancelot did to his castle fare;
The battle was over but truth to say,
There was sorrow and weeping sore;
The battle had been no child's play.

266

Into all lands both north and south
The word of this battle had sprung;
In Rome they knew it was the truth
That England had sorrow so strong;
For this the Pope he had much ruth;
A letter sealed he with his hand
Saying that peace must be made in truth,
Or under interdict would be the land.

267

There was a bishop there at Rome
From Rochester this worthy man was,
To England as a messenger he did come
To Carlisle where King Arthur was;
The Pope's letter he did there unfold
In the castle before the dais;
He bade them obey the Pope in Rome
And keep England in rest and peace.

268

When all there had the letter seen
They knew the words the Pope did make:
The king must take again the queen
And make accord with Lancelot du Lake;
A peace must be made there between
Forevermore, and truce must he make
Or England under interdict would be
And turned to sorrow for their sake.

269

The king against this could not be;
He must do the Pope's commandment.
Happy he'd be to have the queen,
If saving England it meant.
But Gawayne was of a heart so keen
That never would he assent
That ever should there accord be
While he in life still went.

270

The other lords though did agree,
And the king then did a letter make;
The bishop served as go-between
To Sir Lancelot du Lake,
And asked him if he would the queen
Courteously to King Arthur take,
Or England under interdict would be
And turned to sorrow for their sake.

271

Lancelot answered courteously
As a knight both hardy and keen:
"In many a battle I stood," said he,
"Both for the king and for the queen;
Destroyed would his best towers be
If there to help I had not been;
With little honor he repays me
For all the years that I served him."

272

The bishop spoke then without fail
And with scarcely a moment's thought:
"Sir, won thou many a battle
Through grace that in thee God had wrought.
Thou shall do now as I counsel;
Think of Him and what His suffering taught.
Sir, women are by nature frail;
Let not England for this go to nought!"

273

"Sir Bishop, castles for to hold,
Know thee well, I have no need.
I might be king, if that I would
Of the whole of Benwick indeed,
And I could ride my lands so bold
With my knights all straight on steed,
But if I yield the queen as thou say I should
Then for her life I have great dread."

274

"By Mary, of all maids the flower,
And by God that rules as is right,
The queen shall have no dishonor;
To this my word I shall plight.
Brought she'll be into her bower
To her ladies and maidens bright,
And held will she be in more honor
Than ever she was by day or night."

275

"Now if I do grant such a thing,
If deliver the queen I do,
Sir Bishop, tell my lord the king,
Gawayne and the others too,
That they must first give me pledging
Of truce between our parties two."

276

The bishop was happy as man could be
That this was Lancelot's answer,
And quickly mounted his palfrey
And to Carlisle did he fare.
And soon the tidings there told he
Of what Sir Lancelot's words were.
The king and court then happily
Pledged a truce and wrought it there.

277

With the assent of one and all
A strong truce there they wrought.
Though Gawayne was of heart so keen
Against the truce he said nought,
And keep him to this truce would he
While Lancelot the queen home brought.
But peace between them would not be
Ere each the other's death had sought.

278

A goodly truce then did they make
And with their seals was it bound,
And then three bishops they did take,
The wisest that were in the land,
And sent them to Lancelot du Lake;
At Joyous Gard they there him found,
And the letters then he did take
And the truce he pledged with raised hand.

279

The bishops then went on their way
To Carlisle where the king was at rest.
Lancelot came the following day
With the lady riding abreast.
He had prepared a rich array
As well thou may have guessed.
A hundred knights, and truth to say,
Of all his host these were the best.

280

Lancelot and the queen were clad
In fair robes that were rich indeed,
Of white silk cloth with silver spread,
On ivory saddle and white steed
With saddle cloths of that same thread
That in the heathen lands was made.
Lancelot the queen's palfrey led,
As said the romance I did read.

281

The other knights each and every one
In green silk from the heathen land
And without armor rode alone,
And each knight wore a green garland,
And their saddles gleamed with rich stone;
Each had an olive branch in hand,
And all the field around them shone,
And as they rode they loudly sang.

282

To the castle then came they
At the palace did they alight;
The queen Lancelot took from her palfrey;
All thought it was a seemly sight.
And then the king saluted he
As a man of much great might;
Many fair words then spoke they,
But weeping there stood many a knight.

283

Lancelot then these words did speak
To the king of such great might:
"Sir, to thee have I brought thy queen;
I have saved her life with the right.
She is a lady fair, I ween,
And true she has been day and night.
If any man says she is not clean
I proffer me therefore to fight."

284

Then answered Arthur to him there
With words that were fierce and slow:
"Lancelot, I thought that nevermore
I would through thee suffer such woe,
So dear we to each other were;
Nevertheless, thou was my foe,
But in spite of this it grieves me sore
That ever was war between us two."

285

Lancelot then answered he
When he had listened long:
"Sir, for thy trouble thou blame me
And well thou do know that is wrong.
I was never far from thee
When thou had any trouble strong,
But to liar's lies listened thee
And from this all woe has sprung."

286

Then to Lancelot spoke Gawayne,
Who was a hardy knight and free:
"Deny it not, t'would be in vain,
That thou has slain my brothers three;
Therefore shall we prove our main
In field of battle," said he.
"Until one of us has the other slain,
Happy shall I never be."

287

Lancelot answered with heart so sore,
For this he had not sought;
"Gawayne," he said, "Though I was there
Myself, thy brothers slew I nought;
Many other knights there were
That since then their lives have lost."
Lancelot sighed wonder sore
And tears to his eyes were brought.

288

Lancelot then sadly spoke he
To the king and Sir Gawayne:
"Sir, shall there never accord be
So that friends we might be again?"
Then spoke Gawayne most bitterly,
That knight of might and main:
"Nay, accord shall thou never see
Til one of us has the other slain."

289

"Since it never may betide
That peace between us shall be,
May I into my own lands ride
In safety with my knights so keen?
Then here will I no longer bide
But leave will I take of thee.
Wherever I wend in the world so wide
England no more will I see."

290

Then King Arthur answered there,
And the tears from his eyes did run,
"By Jesus Christ," the king then swore,
"Who all this world wrought and won,
Go to thy lands when thou will fare;
Shall stop thee no living man!"
He said, "Alas!" with sighing sore,
"That ever yet this war began."

291

"Now that I shall go away
To the lands that are my home,
May I there in safety stay
Or will thou there against me come?"
Sir Gawayne then said he "Nay,
By Him that made the sun and moon,
Prepare as well as ever thou may
For after thee will we come full soon."

292

Lancelot then his leave took there;
    For no longer would he bide.
His palfrey then he did prepare
And made himself ready to ride.
Then with his knights out did he fare,
And down their faces tears did slide.
Sorrow there was and weeping sore,
At this parting was little pride.

293

To Joyous Gard that castle fair
Rode Lancelot and his noble knights;
There they readied themselves to fare
As men who were of much great might;
Out they rode with banner and spear,
And stopped they neither day nor night
Til to Caerleon came they there,
Where ships for them were ready right.

294

Then out they shipped upon the flood,
Lancelot and those that with him went.
Weather had they fair and good,
And their will it was ever to wend
Quick to their haven where it stood,
And where they their lives would spend.
Indeed, full happy was their mood
When Jesus them to Benwick sent.

295

There they arrived upon the strand
And folk were glad to see them there;
The greatest lords of all the land
To Sir Lancelot did they fare.
They knelt and kissed his foot and hand
And for their lord they took him there.
By his judgments would they stand
And loyalty to him did they swear.

296

Lancelot made Bors king of Gawnes
As that was both law and his right;
Lionel he made king of France,
Gaul it was called in olden time;
All his folk he did advance
And lands he gave to every knight,
And prepared his castles for mischance
For he knew he would have to fight.

297

Ector he crowned with his own hand,
So the French book tells us true,
And made him king of his father's land
And set him over all to rule.
Of that land Ector king did stand,
And worthy he was as men knew.
But nothing for himself he planned,
For to live in peace would Lancelot do.

298

Arthur would no longer abide,
Night and day his heart was sore;
Messengers he sent to ride,
And through all England did they fare
To earls and barons on every side
To tell them that they should prepare
On Sir Lancelot's lands to ride
To burn and slay and make all bare.

299

Then Arthur gathered all his knights
And a council then did he make;
He bade them to choose as they might
He who the best steward would make
To rule when Arthur left to fight,
And who would be best for Britain's sake,
For greatly was the king in fright
That foreigners the land would take.

300

Then the knights spoke courteously
And said that in truth they thought
That Sir Mordred the best would be,
Even if through all the land they sought,
To keep the realm in truce and peace.
Then was the book before him brought
And Mordred as steward chose he.
Little knew they then what they'd wrought.

301

No longer then did they there bide,
But with much haste did they prepare,
And when they were ready for to ride
Out they went with banner and spear
And forth they rode with much pride,
Til to Caerleon came they there,
And waiting for them by the sea side
Were great galleys of fashion fair.

302

Out they shipped upon the sea
And sailed they over the water wide,
And then when Benwick they did see
With force against it they did ride.
Withstood them neither stone nor tree;
They burnt and slew on every side.
Lancelot was in his best city,
There the battle would he abide.

303

Lancelot then his knights called he,
His earls and his barons bold,
And he bade them there to agree,
For of their will would he be told;
Should they attack the host, asked he,
Or should they their castle walls hold?
For Arthur's fierceness they could see
Was a threat they would soon behold.

304

Bors de Gawnes that noble knight
Sternly spoke he there:
"Know ye now all men of might,
That to test thy honor thou must prepare;
With spear and shield and armor bright
Against the foe must we ride there;
King and duke and earl and knight
We shall them beat and to ground bear."

305

Then spoke Lionel at that time
Who of war was wise and bold:
"My lords, I advise that we do bide
And that our castle walls we hold;
Let them attack with all their pride
Til they are both hungry and cold,
Then shall we out upon them ride
And cut them down like sheep in the fold."

306

Sir Bangdemagew, that bold king
To Lancelot spoke at that time:
"Sir, courtesy and your suffering
Have given us woe full wide;
Now think thee well upon this thing
For if over our lands they ride,
All to nought they might us bring
While in holes we here do hide."

307

Then Galehod who was so good,
To Lancelot spoke he there:
"Sir, here are knights of royal blood
Who are ready to fight and dare;
Give me leave for Cross on Rood,
With my men against Arthur to fare;
Though like fierce madmen fight they could
I shall slay them and plunder them bare."

308

Of North Wales were brothers seven
Full great of strength and pride,
And few there were who could ever
Against them in battle bide.
And with one voice they all said then:
"My lords, how long will you take to decide?
Lancelot, for God's love in heaven,
With Galehod forth let us ride!"

309

Then spoke he whose words did all attend,
Himself, Sir Lancelot du Lake:
"Here should we stay I recommend
And over our walls a watch take,
And to Arthur will I a message send
That says truce with him would we make;
If he his courtesy would lend
Then I hope that peace we can make.

310

"Though well we might with honor win
For one thing is my heart sore;
This land is filled with folk full thin
And battles have left the land bare.
Know ye well it is a sin
For Christian folk to slay thus more.
With mildness then we shall begin
Then God shall show us how to fare."

311

And in assent to this all were
And watch then did they take,
These knights as fierce as any boar
And dreadful as a fire-drake.
A damsel did they summon there
And hastily letters did they make,
For she should with the message fare
That they with Arthur a truce would make.

312

That maiden she was fair to view
When she upon her steed was set;
Her apparel was all one hue
Made all of rich green velvet,
In her hand a branch green and new;
No one to her would offer threat;
By the branch men messengers knew
Whenever they with them met.

313

Lodged was King Arthur in a field
By a river broad and wide,
And there she paused and she beheld
Pavilions that were set on high;
There was many a comely tent
That gleamed like gold to the sight,
And on one hung King Arthur's shield
And to that tent the maid drew nigh.

314

King Arthur's banner out was set
On the tent to which she drew near,
And there a knight full soon she met
Called Sir Lucan de Botteler,
And she from him did greeting get,
That maid of full mild cheer.
Her errand she did not forget,
She told him she was a messenger.

315

Sir Lucan then did down her take
And forth did he her lead,
And kindly to her then he spake
As a courteous knight indeed.
"Thou comes from Lancelot du Lake,
The best that ever bestrode steed;
May Jesus for His Mother's sake
Give thee the grace well to speed."

316

Fair was it set upon the plain
That pavilion of rich apparel;
The king himself and Sir Gawayne
Together sat in its hall.
Before the king then kneeled the maid
And low to the ground did she fall;
Her letters then she gave the twain
And soon were they read by all.

317

Then well and fair the maiden spake,
Sir Lancelot's case did she plead:
"Sir, God save thee from woe and wrake
And all thy knights," said she.
"Greets thee well, Lancelot du Lake
Who to thy word did ever heed;
A twelve month truce he would have thee make
That peaceful life here he might lead.

318

"And then, sir, if thou should decree,
He will promise with upraised hand
That to a peace he will agree,
And stable he will ever stand;
He will then go full hastily
And mildly to the Holy Land,
And there will he stay says he
As long as he is living man."

319

The king then called to counsel
His knights so noble and keen;
First he said, without any fail:
"Methinks that noble terms these be;
He'd be a fool, without any fail
For such fair advances to flee."
The king the maiden then did tell:
"'Tis sad that war between us should be."

320

"Nay, in truth!" said Sir Gawayne,
"Enough woe has he brought me now.
That traitor has my brothers slain.
All for thy love, sir, that is truth!
Home will I not return again
Til he be dead hanged from a bough.
While I have either might or main
To face him in battle I vow!"

321

The king reluctant seemed to be
And almost every lord made it plain
That all then wanted to have peace;
All agreed but Sir Gawayne;
To fight with Lancelot vowed he
Or never to go home again.
Arthur the war could not then cease
Because of his vows to Gawayne.

322

The king had come into the hall
And in his royal seat he sat;
He sent a knight the maid to call,
Sir Lucan de Botteler was that,
"Tell Lancelot and his knights all
That a vow I made holds me yet,
And stop us not will any wall
Until with force we have them met."

323

The maiden then had her answer,
And sadly she prepared to ride,
Her fair palfrey was readied there
And on her way she set aright.
And through the forest she did fare,
And hasted her with all her might
Where Lancelot and his knights were
In Benwick that city bright.

324

Then came she back within the wall,
That worthy maiden, fair indeed,
With grace she came into the hall;
A knight took her down off her steed.
Then to the princes one and all
She gave the letters for to read.
They did not then a council call
But quickly prepared for their need.

325

As men that eager were to fight
From the field would they never flee,
But in the morn when it was light
Around them their foe did they see;
Each man stationed in manner right,
A mighty host they seemed to be.

326

Early when the day did spring
The trumpeters on the walls went,
And there they saw a wondrous thing,
Rich pavilions, many a tent,
And Sir Arthur, that noble king
From there his folk he sent
To make attack without ceasing,
And against the walls their bows they bent.

327

Lancelot astonished was he
By the folk before the castle wall,
But rather this would he then see
Than unknowing send out his knights all.
He said, "Now, princes, hold thy peace,
For many things may yet befall;
If they will not their sieging cease,
Regret it they will one and all."

328

Then Gawayne who was good at every need
Clad himself in his best armor
And quickly jumped upon a steed
That in battle had much power;
And forth he sprang like a spark indeed
To the gates before the tower,
And challenged he any knight to speed
And in combat prove his honor.

329

Bors de Gawnes then came he down
Upon a steed strong and fair;
With helm and shield and hauberk brown,
And in his hand a mighty spear;
Out rode this knight of much renown.
Gawayne showed he knew much of war
For horse and man both bore he down
With a great blow that he struck there.

330

Sir Lionel was all ready then,
For his brother had he much woe,
And readily with his steed out ran
And against Gawayne did he go.
Gawayne finished what he began
And fiercely he fought his foe,
Til down he bore both horse and man;
And every day some served he so.

331

And so for more than half a year
As long as they there did remain
Every day might men see there
Men wounded and some slain;
None knew how ever thus it were
That such good grace had Sir Gawayne,
For ever he stayed whole and fair
And all against him fought in vain.

332

Then it befell upon a time
Sir Gawayne who was bold and free
Made himself ready for to ride
Before the gates of that city.
Lancelot was a traitor he cried,
And slain he had his brothers three;
This Lancelot could not abide,
Lest called coward ever he'd be.

333

The lord that was great of honor,
Himself, Sir Lancelot du Lake,
Above the gates upon the tower
Courteously to the king spake:
"My lord, God save thy honor!
And sorry am I for thy sake
Against thy kin to stand this hour
But now I must this challenge take."

334

Lancelot armed himself full well,
For truth to say he had great need;
Helm and hauberk were all of steel
And he bestrode a mighty steed.
Nothing he lacked, as I thee tell.
Much good armor had he indeed
And mighty weapons for to wield
When forth he sprang with fiercesome speed.

335

Ordered were all the knights on high
That no matter how it should fare
No man should to them come nigh
Til one died or surrendered there.
Then all withdrew who'd been nearby
And on the field so broad and bare
The two met beneath the blue sky,
And many blows exchanged full sore.

336

Gawayne had been granted the grace
Through a holy father's boon,
That when he was in any place
Where he should battle do,
That all his strength would grow apace
From the morning time until noon.
So Lancelot, such was the case,
Against twenty strokes gave he none.

337

Lancelot saw there was no succor,
And that he his time must bide,
And many blows he did endure
Until it grew near to noontide.
And then became he straight and sure
And to Gawayne gave a wound wide;
Over his face the blood did pour
And down he fell upon his side.

338

Through the helm into the head
Was hardy Gawayne wounded so,
That almost was his life then sped;
On foot he might no further go,
But still his sword he would not shed
For never fear did Gawayne know.
Away from him stepped Lancelot then,
He would not strike another blow.

339

Back drew Lancelot from his side
And looked he down on Sir Gawayne,
And then that knight cried loud and high:
"Traitor and coward, come again!
When I am whole and ready to ride
Again will I fight with might and main,
And yet if now thou would come nigh,
Know well thou shall that I'm not slain!"

340

"Gawayne, while thou did stiffly stand,
Many a blow today of thee I stood;
And I forbore thee in every land
For love and that thou were Arthur's blood;
When thou are whole in heart and hand
Change thy mind and turn home thou should.
While I am Lancelot and living man,
God shield me from such madness if He would!

341

"But have good day, my lord the king,
And so too thy noble knights all;
Go now home and leave thy warring;
Ye win no honor at this wall,
And if I should my knights outbring
I know that rue it sore thou shall;
Lord, therefore think about this thing
And how many folks thus might fall."

342

Lancelot who was much of main
Boldly to his castle went;
The good knights that were of his train
With cries of joy to him then went.
King Arthur's party took Gawayne
And cared for his wounds in his tent.
But ere he recovered might and main
From his body life was nearly spent.

343

For a fortnight, truth to say,
Near to his death and sore unsound
Sir Gawayne in his bed there lay
Before he was healed of his wound.
Then it befell upon a day
That he dressed him in armor sound
And to the gate he took his way;
To challenge Lancelot was he bound.

344

"Come Lancelot and prove thy main,
Thou traitor that has treason wrought;
My three brothers have thou slain,
And falsely have them to ground brought.
While I still have might and main
This quarrel will I never leave aught;
No peace ever shall there be seen
Ere to the death we have fought."

345

Lancelot thought it nothing good,
For Gawayne's words gave him much sorrow,
And he before the gates then stood
And to King Arthur spoke he so:
"Sir, much I rue that Gawayne should
So loudly proclaim me his foe,
None will blame me, by Cross on Rood,
If slay him in battle I do."

346

Lancelot readied himself to come down
And boldly the battle abide
With helm and shield and hauberk brown,
None better in the whole world wide,
And at his side his sword was bound,
His spear and banner he held high,
And full quickly then came he down
When ready he was for to ride.

347

Gawayne gripped a good strong spear
And in he glided glad and gay;
Lancelot showed he know much of war
For soon did he lead the way;
So stoutly against each other did they bear
That a marvel it was, truth to say,
What blows they gave each other there
And what deep wounds gave and took they.

348

When near at hand was the time of noon
Gawayne's strength began to increase,
So bitterly his blows were strewn
That Lancelot a-wearied was;
But then his sword he gripped anon
And as Gawayne would not cease,
Such a blow he smote him then
That all who saw were ill at ease.

349

Forward then did Lancelot bound
And as Gawayne still would not cease,
Through his helm then that was rich and round
His noble sword did cleave.
Gawayne was hit on his old wound
And over the saddle he went;
Grimly he groaned upon the ground
And lay in shame and in torment.

350

Yet while in swooning there he lay
Gripped he still his sword and shield;
"Lancelot," he said, "truth to say,
By Him that does all power wield,
While in me lasts my life today,
To thee shall I never yield;
Do the worst that ever thou may,
I shall defend me in the field."

351

Lancelot then full still he stood,
As a man that was much of might;
"Gawayne, in my mind I rue
That men hold thee so noble a knight.
Think thou that be so mad I would
As against a feeble man to fight?
I will not now, by Cross on Rood,
Nor never did by day or night.

352

"But have good day, my lord the king
And so too all thy noble men;
Go now home and leave thy warring,
For here no honor will thou win;
And if I should my knights out bring
I know full soon that would be seen.
Now think, good lord, upon that thing
For the love that between us has been."

353

It was longer than months two,
As I do understand,
Ere Gawayne to walk or ride could go
Or had foot upon earth to stand.
For a third time he was ready though
To do battle with heart and hand;
But a message to them came now
That they must home to England.

354

A message had to them been brought
And no man there thought it good;
The king himself with sorrow thought,
And much did he mourn and brood.
For treason had in England been wrought,
And return he must over the flood.
They broke their siege and home they sought
In bitter and in angry mood.

355

That false traitor, Sir Mordred,
The king's sister's son was he,
And his own son too, as I read,
And therefore chosen as steward was he;
But falsely had he England led.
Know thee well and listen to me,
His uncle's wife would Mordred wed,
And all knew that would evil be.

356

Gave he many a festive meal
And many gifts gave he also;
Men said with him was joy and weal,
And with Arthur sorrow and woe.
And thus then right to wrong did go,
And the illness would not itself heal;
And then before long seemed it so
That to Mordred did all men kneel.

357

False letters then he had him wrought
And sent messengers them to bring,
That Arthur had to death been brought,
And choose they must another king.
And then many men spoke their thought:
"Arthur loved he nought but warring
And such things were all he sought;
It is right that thus he took his ending."

358

Mordred then called a parliament
And the people thither did come,
And wholly with their free assent
They made Mordred king with crown
At Canterbury, far in Kent;
A fortnight held he the feast in town,
And after that to Winchester he went,
A rich bridal feast to set down.

359

In summer when it was fair and bright
His father's wife then would he wed;
Her would he hold with main and might
And so bring her as bride to bed.
She prayed him leave of a fortnight,
For much was that lady in dread;
To London she asked for leave to ride
To clad her and her maids, she said.

360

The queen white as a lily flower
With many knights that were her kin
Went to London to the tower
And barred the gates and dwelled within.
Mordred lost all his color,
And there went but came he not in;
With arrows the walls he did shower,
But entrance he never did win.

361

The Archbishop of Canterbury thither rode
And his cross before him brought;
He said: "Sir, for Cross on Rood,
What have thee now in thy thought?
Your father's wife, this must be understood,
To wed with her, sir, may you nought;
If Arthur comes over the flood
Then dearly will this deed be bought!"

362

"Thou foolish clerk," Sir Mordred said,
"Think thou thus to thwart my will?
By Him that for us suffered pain,
These words shall thou soon like full ill!
Thou shall be drawn apart by horses twain
And hanged high upon a hill!"
The bishop fled, he dared not complain,
And let him his follies fulfill.

363

Then he cursed him with book and bell
At Canterbury far in Kent.
And when Mordred of this heard tell,
Men to seek the bishop he sent.
There no more dared the bishop dwell,
So gold and silver took he then;
To stay there longer was not well,
So to a wilderness he went.

364

And there the world he did forsake
And thought he of joy nevermore.
But there a chapel did he make
Between two high forests hoar.
There he a hermit's ways did take
And clothing of black he wore,
And often he did weep and wake
For England that had sorrows sore.

365

Mordred had lain in siege full long
But the tower he could not win,
Neither with strength nor battle strong
Nor by any means could he come in.
Arthur he feared, he knew his wrong
But he would not desist from his sin.
He planned to deny any wrong
To the kingdom that he was crowned in.

366

Forth to Dover he did ride,
And to the sea-coast there he went;
To earls and barons on every side
Great gifts he gave and letters sent.
He blocked the sea on every side
With many bold men with bows bent.
For England that is broad and wide
From his own father he would defend.

367

King Arthur who was great of might,
With his folk came over the flood;
A hundred galleys fair to sight
Filled with barons bold and high of blood
He planned to land as was his right
At Dover; this he thought was good,
But there he found many a hardy knight
That against him in battle stood.

368

Arthur soon did take the land
That his foe had tried to defend;
Of those that against him did stand
Was many a one he'd thought his friend.
Then was the king a maddened man
As with his men up he did wend;
So strong they fought upon that strand
That many a man met his end.

369

Gawayne into the fight did bound,
But, alas! Too long his head was bare;
He was still sick and sore unsound
And his wounds grieved him yet full sore.
A blow he took on his old wound
From the handle of an oar,
And good Gawayne he went to ground
And speech he spoke nevermore.

370

Many bold men with their bows bent
Boldly up to the boats did go,
And rich hauberks they cut and rent
From which burst out the rich red blood.
Sharp edged spears through many went;
These games they thought not good,
And by the time of the battle's end
With bloody waters ran the flood.

371

Arthur was so much of might
None there were who him withstood;
His sword hewed through their helms so bright,
And from their wounds flowed the blood.
And then when ended was the fight,
The false were felled, and some had fled
To Canterbury on that night
To warn their master Sir Mordred.

372

Mordred rode from Canterbury town,
Boldly would he battle abide.
With helm and shield and hauberk brown
All his company forth did ride.
They met the king at Barlam Down
Full early in the morning time;
With banners bright and weapons sound
Against Arthur's men did they ride.

373

Arthur's troop was in rich array,
And their horns blew loud on high;
And Mordred he seemed glad and gay
But a traitor he was, false in fight.
They fought throughout that whole long day
Until the night was almost nigh;
And those who saw it they did say
That ne'er had they seen such a sight.

374

King Arthur fought with heart so good,
Nobler knight than he was there none.
Through helms into heads did weapons go
And knights were stirred in blood and bone.
Mordred was like a madman in his mood,
He called his folk and told each one:
"Save thyself, for Cross on Rood!
Alas, this day for us is done!"

375

Many men lay on the banks so bare,
Dead of the blows they had borne;
Many brave deeds had been done there,
But dead now was many a lord.
Mordred was full of sorrow and care
At Canterbury the next morn,
But Arthur on the field stayed there
With his noble knights at the fore.

376

Early in the morning time
Arthur bade his horns to blow,
And his folk he called from every side,
And the dead they buried in a row
In pits that were deep and wide;
And on each grave a mound did go
So that when men thereby would ride
The dead by their marks they would know.

377

Arthur went to his dinner then
And all his folk followed him fast;
But when the king found Sir Gawayne
In a ship lying dead by a mast,
Ere he recovered might or main,
Nearly from life he passed.

378

They laid Gawayne upon a bier
And to a castle they him bore,
And in the choir in the chapel there
They buried him with hearts full sore.
King Arthur then lost all his cheer
What wonder he was sad therefore;
His sister's son to him so dear
The king would not see evermore.

379

No longer there would Arthur bide,
For there he had only bad rest,
And went he forth by the south side
And then towards Wales went he west;
At Salisbury he thought to bide,
At that time he thought that was best,
And call to him at Whitsuntide
Bold barons to do his behest.

380

Unto him came many a mighty knight
For wide in the world the word had sprung
That Sir Arthur had all the right
And Mordred warred on him with wrong.
Frightening it was to see with sight
Arthur's host so broad and long,
But Mordred who was much of might
With great gifts meanwhile made him strong.

381

Soon after the feast of the Trinity
Was a battle between them set;
A bitter battle that would be
One that men would never forget.
Sir Arthur then made games and glee
For gladness that they should be met,
And Mordred came into the country
With those he from afar did get.

382

That night when Arthur went to bed
To rest for the battle on morrow,
With strange dreams was he beset
Of many that would have sorrow.
He dreamed that he sat in gold all clad,
And on his head was his crown,
Upon a wheel that full wide spread
And there were his knights all around.

383

The wheel was fair and rich and round,
Never was there one half so high,
And there he sat full richly crowned
And many coins and jewels had he;
Then down he looked upon the ground,
And black water he there did see
With dragons so fierce that lay unbound
That no man to them dared come nigh.

384

Then was he much afraid to fall
Among those fiends that there fought.
And then the wheel did turn with all
And by each limb dragons him caught.
The king then loud did cry and call
Like a man with his wits distraught;
His chamberlains then waked him all
And out of his dream was he brought.

385

All night the king did wail and weep,
With dreary heart and voice of pain,
And then near dawn he fell asleep
And dreamed he of Sir Gawayne;
He thought Gawayne he then did meet
With more folk than men could name
By a river that was broad and deep;
All seemed like angels that from heaven came.

386

Much pleasure then did Arthur gain
When his sister's son he did see;
"Welcome," he said, "Sir Gawayne,
If thou are alive glad I be.
Now beloved friend, tell me plain
Who are these folk that follow thee?"
"In truth, sir," then said Sir Gawayne,
"They bide in bliss where I might be.

387

"Ladies fair and lords they were
Who from this world now have gone;
While I yet had my life to spend
Against their foes for them I fought.
Now they think me their greatest friend
And bless the time that I was born.
They asked if with me they could wend
To meet with thee upon this morn.

388

"A month's truce, Uncle, must thou take
Before thou fight," said Sir Gawayne,
"To help thee will come Lancelot du Lake
With many men of might and main;
Tomorrow the battle thou must forsake
Or else truly thou shall be slain."
With woe the king did then awake
And cried, "Alas, this rueful reign!"

389

Hastily then dress he did
And to all his lords he did say:
"With strange dreams have I been beset
And now nothing could make me gay;
We must unto Sir Mordred send,
And the battle set for another day,
Or else with shame will I be met;
This knew I in bed as I lay.

390

"Go thou, Sir Lucan de Botteler,
Thou who wise words can unfold,
And with thee be sure to take there
Many bishops and barons bold."
Then forth they went, I tell thee fair,
As in the true books it is told,
To Mordred and his knights where they were,
At least a hundred knights all told.

391

These knights that were great of valor,
Before Sir Mordred then they stood,
They greeted him with great honor,
As barons bold and high of blood:
"Greetings to thee sends King Arthur,
And he prays of thee with mild mood,
That for a month the battle thou defer
For love of He that died on Rood."

392

Mordred who was keen and bold
Became fierce as a boar at bay,
He swore by Judas who Jesus sold:
"Such sayings are not now to say;
To what he has vowed he shall hold,
And one of us shall die this day;
And tell him too that this I told:
I shall destroy him if I may."

393

"Sir," they said, "without lie,
Though you are both to battle bound,
Many a knight is sure to die
By the blows struck on that Down;
Yet were it better not to vie.
Let him be king and bear the crown,
And after his day has gone by
You shall rule England, tower and town."

394

Mordred then stood still a while,
And then his eyes up went:
"This might be well if 'twere his will
To give me Cornwall and Kent!
Let us meet upon yonder hill
And talk together with good intent;
Certain terms there we may fulfill,
And to that, sirs, I will assent.

395

"And if we may with speeches speed
All these matters in detail,
And if then is agreement made
To give me Kent and Cornwall
With my fealty shall he be paid;
But if then these discussions fail,
Arthur may leap upon his steed
And prepare there to do battle."

396

"Sir, will thou come in such manner
With twelve knights or fourteen
Or with all thy strength come there
With helmets bright and weapons keen?"
"Nay, in truth," said Mordred there,
"No more will I bring than fourteen;
But both our armies should be near
And we shall meet in between."

397

Then the knights did take their leave
And swiftly on their way they went,
And back they rode as they did please
Where Arthur sat within his tent:
"Sir," said they, "we have proffered peace,
If thou will but thereto assent
To leave him thy crown after thy days
And in thy life Cornwall and Kent.

398

"If to this behest ye will hold,
And thy troth truly thereto plight
Then make ready thy men so bold
With helm and sword and hauberk bright;
Ye shall meet on yonder knoll
That either host may see with sight,
And if this accord fails to hold
There will be nought to do but fight."

399

Then when Arthur the news heard he
And truly thereto had he sworn,
Then his host he did array
With broad banners before them borne
All gleaming as bright as the day
When they did meet upon the morn;
No man lives who ever did see
A fairer sight than this before.

400

But Mordred had many men more,
Sir Mordred of might and main,
He had twelve against Arthur's two
Of barons bold in might and main.
Arthur and Mordred both had it so
That they would meet upon the plain
The better to come to and fro
To make their accord, truth to say.

401

In his heart thought Arthur thus,
And to his lords he then did say:
"Yonder traitor I do not trust,
For falsely he may us betray
While accord we do discuss;
If any weapon there draw they
Then bravely attack them we must,
Til he and all his host we slay."

402

Mordred who was keen and thorough
Spoke to his knights that morn:
"I know that Arthur has much woe,
From loss of his lands is he forlorn;
With fourteen knights and with no more
We shall meet at yonder thorn,
But if treason between us go
Then forth shall our banners be borne."

403

Arthur with his knights fourteen
Their way on foot to the thorn they wound;
With helm and shield and hauberk keen
Bravely they walked across the ground;
But when the parley did begin
An adder glided forth upon the ground;
He stung a knight, and men could see
That he became sick and unsound.

404

Out he drew his sword so bright,
To kill that adder was his thought;
When Arthur's party saw that sight
Their weapons up they caught;
Then nothing could withstand their might,
They thought that treason had been wrought.
That day died many a brave knight
And many a man was brought to nought.

405

Arthur upon his steed leaped he
And nothing could withstand his might;
Mordred was out of his wits nearly
And like a madman he did fight.
Of their accord then was nothing seen
But shattered spears and injured knights,
And many a man, brave of deed,
To the ground went ere it was night.

406

Mordred wounded many a man
And boldly did the battle abide;
And out his steed so fiercely ran
That over many he did ride;
And King Arthur, that mighty man,
Dealt he wounds wicked and wide
From the morning that the fight began
Until it was almost evntide.

407

In battle was that whole day spent
And many a fierce word was spake,
Many a sword was bowed and bent,
And many a helm they did break;
Shining helms they cut and rent
As battle there they did make.
A hundred thousand to the ground were sent
And the boldest were there made meek.

408

Not since Brutus out of Troy had sought
And made in Britain his own home,
Had such wonders ever been wrought,
Never yet under the sun.
By evening, living were there nought
That ever stirred with blood and bone;
Only Arthur and two that he had brought
And Mordred were living alone.

409

One was Lucan de Botteler
Who bled from many a baleful wound,
And his brother, Sir Bedivere
Who was sorely sick and unsound.
Then spoke King Arthur these words there:
"Shall we not bring this thief to ground?"
And fiercely then he gripped his spear,
And at each other the two did bound.

410

He struck Mordred in the breast
And the spear through his body did bore,
And Mordred there his life he lost,
And speech he spoke nevermore.
As he died, up his arms he cast
And gave Arthur a wound so sore
That pierced his head through helm and crest,
And Arthur swooned three times or more.

411

Sir Lucan and Sir Bedivere
Between them the king they upheld,
Then forth with Arthur went that pair.
All the slain lay in the field,
And the noble king to them so dear
For pain his body could not wield.
A chapel they found and went in there,
No other place had they beheld.

412

At night they in the chapel lay
By the seaside, as I thee tell;
To Mary for mercy they did cry
And with dreary hearts their prayers did tell,
And to her dear Son did they pray:
"Jesus Christ, who loved men well,
Teach his soul to know the right way
To find heaven's bliss if he may."

413

As Sir Lucan de Botteler stood,
Folks to the plain came nigh,
And the bold barons of bone and blood
They robbed while there they did lie.
To the king Lucan came as fast as he could
To warn him with words so sly.

414

Near the king he stood full still
And ruefully spoke he:
"Sir, I have been to yonder hill,
And drawn there many folk be;
I know not if they mean us good or ill,
But I advise we go," said he.
"If it is now thy worthy will
That to some nearby town go we."

415

"Now, Sir Lucan," Arthur then said,
"Lift me up while yet I last."
Then both his arms on him he spread
With all his strength to hold him fast;
The king from his wounds so badly he bled
That swoon he did with eyes upcast;
Sir Lucan he was hard beset
But held him til his own heart burst at last.

416

When Arthur from swooning recovered there
By an altar up he stood;
Sir Lucan who to him was dear
Lay still and dead in his own blood.
His bold brother, Sir Bedivere
Mourned and was full sad;
To his brother he came not near,
But wept like one gone mad.

417

The king then turned from where he stood
To Bedivere with these words keen;
"Take Excalibur, my sword so good,
A better one was never seen;
Go cast it in the salty flood,
And a great wonder will be seen.
Hie thee fast, by Cross on Rood,
And tell me what thou there have seen."

418

Then went the knight so brave and free;
To save the sword he would be glad.
He thought: "Would it better be
If no man after this sword had?
How can I cast it in the sea?
Never on earth was man so made."
And the sword he hid under a tree,
And said: "Sir, I did as ye bade."

419

"What saw thou there?" then asked the king,
"Tell me now, if thou can."
"Truly, sir," he said, "Nothing,
But waters deep and waves so wan."
"Ah, thou disobeyed my bidding!
Why have thou done so, thou false man?
A different message thou must bring."
Then forth again the good knight ran.

420

He thought the sword he yet would hide,
And cast the scabbard in the flood;
"If any adventure should betide
"Thereby shall I see token good."
Into the sea did the scabbard slide
And a while on the bank he stood;
Then to the king he came in time
And said: "Sir, tis done by the Rood."

421

"Saw thou any wonder more?"
"Truly, sir, saw I nought."
"Ah, false traitor!" he said there,
"Twice thou have me treason wrought;
And for that shall thou rue full sore;
Such treason shall be dearly bought."
"Mercy," the knight did then implore,
And once again the sword he sought.

422

Bedivere then knew what was best
And straight to the sword he did go;
Then into the sea he did it cast
And he watched it as it did go;
And then out came a hand no less
From the deep water below;
The sword it did seize and brandish
And then vanished beneath the flow.

423

To the king again went he there
And said: "Dear sir, I saw a hand,
Out of the water it came all bare
And thrice it brandished that rich brand."
"Help me now, I must go there."
He led his lord unto that strand
Where a rich ship with mast and oar
Full of ladies now did stand.

424

The ladies who were fair and free
To the king gave a welcome strong,
And one, the most lovely was she,
Sorely wept and her hands she wrung.
"Brother," she said, "Ah, woe is me!
From leeching have thou been too long;
And full greatly does that grieve me
For thy injuries are grievous strong."

425

Sir Bedivere spoke ruefully
Where he stood sore and unsound,
And said: "Whither bound are thee?
And where, my lord, shall thou be found?"
The king with sorry sound spoke he:
"Now to Avalon am I bound,
And there for a while shall I be
Until I am healed of my wound."

426

Then the ship from the shore was brought
And Bedivere saw him no more.
Through all the forest his way he sought
Over hills and through forests hoar.
Of his own life he reckoned nought
And all night he spend in weeping sore.
In early morning found he wrought
A chapel between two forests hoar.

427

To the chapel he took his way
And there he saw a wondrous sight;
He saw that there a hermit did lay
Before a great tomb new and bright
Covered with marble gray
With rich writing adorned aright.
And around the bier, truth to say
A hundred candles shone their light.

428

Unto the hermit he went there
And asked who the tomb was for;
The hermit answered with words fair:
"Of that can I tell little more
Than at midnight came ladies here
And never I knew who they were;
This body they brought upon a bier
And buried it with its wounds sore.

429

"And then they offered coins so bright,
I think a hundred pounds or more,
And bade me pray both day and night
For him buried in this earth hoar,
Unto our Lady both day and night
To help his soul evermore."
The writing then read that good knight
And fell to the ground in sorrow sore.

430

"Hermit," he said, "Without lying,
Here lies my lord for whom I mourn,
Arthur who was the greatest king
That ever was in Britain born.
Now give me some of thy clothing
For Him that bore the crown of thorn,
And allow me to stay til my dying,
That I may ever pray for my lord."

431

In wonder stood this holy man,
Once the Archbishop high he was,
That Mordred caused to flee the land;
And now in the wood dwelled he thus.
Thanked he Jesus with grateful sound
That Bedivere had come in peace,
And welcomed him with heart and hand
To dwell with him without cease.

432

When to Queen Gaynor, the king's wife
The news of that battle came back,
Away she went with ladies five
To Almsbury, holy vows to take,
And there she lived a holy life
And in prayers did she weep and wake.
Never again would she be blithe,
And there wore she clothes white and black.

433

When first news was to Lancelot brought
What wonder that his heart was sore;
His men and friends he swiftly sought
And all of those that with him were.
Their galleys were already wrought
And quickly did they prepare;
To help Arthur was their thought
And make Mordred of bliss full bare.

434

Lancelot had seven kings of fame
And many earls and barons bold;
The number of knights I cannot name
And squires in numbers too great to be told,
And all gleaming bright as a flame.
The wind full well for them did hold,
Then through the grace of God they came
To Dover where was their stronghold.

435

There heard Lancelot in that town,
And the tidings heard he plain,
How they had fought at Barlam Down,
And how buried was Sir Gawayne,
And how Mordred would be king with crown,
And how he and the king had each other slain;
And all that had been to the battle bound
At Salisbury lay dead on the plain.

436

He also heard, I tell no lie,
That which made his heart wondrous sore,
That Queen Gaynor, King Arthur's wife,
Had much suffered from sorrow and care,
So away she went with ladies five;
In Dover, the folk knew not where,
Of if dead she was or still alive.
This made his sorrow much the more.

437

Lancelot called his kings with crown
And Sir Bors stood close at his side;
He said: "My lords, I shall go forth;
By these banks do ye abide
For fifteen days from this morn.
No matter if it should betide
That ye hear of a lord whose life was lost,
To my aid rush ye not to ride."

438

Then had he neither peace nor rest
But forth he went with dreary mood;
For three days he rode towards the west
Like one who knew not bad from good.
Then saw he a tower on the west
Standing near a stream in a wood,
And there he thought it would be best
To stop if he might for some food.

439

As he came through a cloister near
He began to weep like one gone mad,
For a lady he saw of beauty clear
And in nun's clothing was she clad;
Three times the lady did swoon there,
With such strong pain she seemed beset
That many nuns to her came near
And to her chamber was she led.

440

"Mercy, madame," said they all,
"For Jesus that is King of Bliss!
Is there any here in bower or hall
Has angered thee?" "Nay," she said to this.
Lancelot to her she bade them call
And all the nuns and the abbess
And all that lived within the wall,
And in council there she said this:

441

"Abbess, to thee I acknowledge here
That through this very man and me,
For we each other did love dear,
All this sorry war came to be;
My lord is slain who had no peer
And many a knight brave and free.
Therefore for sorrow died I near
As soon as I him did see.

442

"When him I saw, the truth to say
All my heart began to grow cold,
That ever I should see this day
To see so many barons bold
That should for us be slain away;
Our love too dearly was bought and sold.
But God whom all men must obey,
Now has me set where I will hold.

443

"Now set I am in such a place
Where my soul's healing I will abide
Til God sees fit to send me grace
Through mercy of His wounds so wide,
That therefore I may in this place
Repent my sins at this time,
So that I may have sight of His face
At Judgment Day on his right side.

444

"Therefore, Sir Lancelot du Lake,
For my love I now thee pray
That my company thou forsake
And to thy kingdom go thy way;
Peaceful and safe thy realm now make
And find a wife soon as thou may
And love thou well this wife thou take;
God give thee joy together, I pray!

445

"To God I pray, Almighty King,
That he give thee both joy and bliss;
But I beseech of thee one thing
That never again after this
Thou come to me for anything,
Nor send me word, but dwell in bliss;
I pray to God Everlasting
To forgive me what I did amiss."

446

"Now, sweet madame, that would I not do,
Not if all the world for that I had;
Never would I be so untrue
Christ forbid I should do that.

447

"God forbid that ever I should
Against thee do such great unright
While we together in this world
Should lead our lives by day and night!
To God I now this vow will hold,
Your destiny shall be mine aright;
A monk will I be in some house bold
To please Great God in all His might.

448

"To please Great God all that I may
Hereafter shall be my intent,
And ever for thee shall I pray;
In this way shall my life be spent."
"Then will thou so?" the queen did say,
"To this forever will thou consent?"
Lancelot said, "If I said nay,
I should deserve to the stake to be sent.

449

"Worthy to be burnt I were
If I would not take such a life
And live in penance as ye do here,
And suffer for God in sorrow and strife
As together in pleasure lived we ere;
By Mary, Mother, Maid and Wife,
Til hence God sends us with death so dear,
To penance I gladly yield my life.

450

"As swiftly to penance will I take
As I may find any hermit
That will receive me for God's sake;
And I will clothe me in black and white."
The sorrow that both then did make
Never man saw the like of it;
"Madame," then said Lancelot du Lake
"Kiss me and I shall go aright."

451

"Nay," said the queen, "That will I not,
Lancelot, think on that no more,
Now to abstain we must have thought
From what delighted us before;
Let us think of Him that has us bought
And we shall please Him therefore;
Think of this world, how there is nought
But war and strife and battle sore."

452

Why should I longer on this dwell?
With that parted Lancelot and the queen;
But never earthly man could tell
The sorrow that there did begin;
They wrung their hands and loud did yell,
Never was such sorrow seen,
And then in swoon they both down fell.
Any who'd seen this touched would have been.

453

The ladies then with little cheer
Into her chamber the queen they bore,
And all full busy made them there
To help the queen in her sorrow sore;
But many also with Lancelot were
To try to comfort him therefore;
Then when he recovered he took his gear
And left from there with nothing more.

454

Heavy was his heart like lead
And all that he could do was mourn.
"Great God, what shall I do?" he said
"Alas, why was I ever born?"
Away he went and soon had fled
To a forest that was there before.
He hoped that he would soon be dead,
And his rich attire off he tore.

455

All night he wept and his hands did wring
And went about as a madman would;
Then early when the day did spring
He came to a stream where a chapel stood;
He heard a bell there sadly ring
And there went quickly as he could;
A priest there had begun to sing
And mass he heard with sorry mood.

456

The Archbishop was the hermit there
Who once had fled for his works true;
The mass he sang while sighing sore
As his face changed color and hue.
Bedivere had sorrow and care
And there he mourned with much great rue.
After mass it was a whole day more
Til each of them the other knew.

457

When the sorrow was at end
The bishop greeted him there
And courteously to him did attend,
And on his knees then did he fare:
"Sir, ye be welcome as our friend
Unto this chapel on banks bare;
We would be glad if ye would spend
This one night, if ye may no more!"

458

When Lancelot they knew at last
In their arms they did him fold,
And then the story came full fast
Of Arthur and his barons bold.
And his heart almost burst at last
While Sir Bedivere the story told;
And when on Arthur's tomb his eyes he cast,
His carefilled heart then turned all cold.

459

His arms he threw against the wall
Rich and bright they were to see;
Before the hermit he did fall
And humbly kneeled upon his knee;
Then he confessed to his sins all
And prayed he might his brother be,
To serve God in bower and hall,
That Mighty King of Mercy free.

460

That holy man would not refuse him
And was happy to grant his boon;
With gladness he received him then
And thanked he Jesus on His throne.
There he absolved him of his sin,
And made him pure as if sins he had none,
And then he kissed him on cheek and chin
And a habit he gave him to put on.

461

Meanwhile his knights at Dover lay,
Where there he should have come again,
Til it befell upon a day
Sir Lionel of might and main
With fifty lords, the truth to say,
Went to seek his lord, as the books explain;
To London then he took his way
Alas, for woe! There was he slain.

462

Sir Bors no longer would he bide
But readied himself as he could
And bade the host to homeward ride,
God send them wind and weather good!
To seek Lancelot would he ride.
Ector and he different ways took,
And Bors went forth to the west side
As one who knew not bad from good.

463

Full early in the morningtide
In a forest he found a well,
And rode he by the riverside
Til he had sight of a chapel;
There at mass he thought to bide.
He heard a sadly ringing bell
And there Sir Lancelot he spied,
And prayed that he might with him dwell.

464

Ere half a year had come to end
Seven of their fellows came there
Where each had sought to find his friend
With sorry heart and voice so drear;
None had the will away to wend
When of Lancelot they did hear,
But all together stayed they then
As if God in Heaven's will it were.

465

Throughout all of seven year
Lancelot was a priest and mass he sang
And penance made and many a prayer;
This life he thought was nothing long.
Sir Bors and all the others there
Books they read and bells they rang,
And they became so thin and spare
Unrecognizable they were ere long.

466

It fell upon an eventide
That Lancelot sickened wondrous sore;
The bishop called he to his side
And all his fellows less and more;
He said: "Here may I no longer bide;
My baleful blood of life is bare.
What good is it the truth to hide,
My foul flesh now to earth will fare.

467

"But, brothers, I pray ye tonight
That tomorrow when ye find me dead,
Ye place me on a bier aright
And to Joyous Gard then me lead;
For the love of Good God's might
To be buried there I plead;
To that a vow I once did plight,
Alas, I'm sorry that I did."

468

"Mercy, sir," they said all three,
"For His love that died on Rood,
If any evil has grieved thee
Tis but a heaviness of the blood;
Tomorrow shall ye better be;
When were ye but of comfort good?"
Merrily spoke all men but he,
But straight to his bed did he go.

469

He kept the bishop with him until
Of his sins he was shriven clean;
Of all his sins he spoke loud and still
Until shriven he had been.
Then he received with much good will
God, Mary's Son, Maiden clean.
While Bors of weeping never had his fill.
Then to bed they went after this had been.

470

A little while before the day
As the bishop lay in his bed,
Such laughter took him as there he lay
That all who heard were sore adread.
They wakened him for truth to say,
They thought that he was hard beset;
He said: "Alas, and well away,
Why was I out of this dream led?

471

"Alas," he said, "Why came ye nigh?
And why therefore did ye wake me?
For there I Lancelot did spy
With angels thirty-thousand and seven.
And him they did bear up on high,
And for him opened the gates of heaven;
Such a sight I now might see
That none on earth saw ever!"

472

"Sir," they said, "for Cross on Rood,
Put such thoughts as these away;
With Sir Lancelot all is good;
He shall be well by break of day."
Candles they lit and to him did go
And found him dead, and truth to say,
He was as fair of flesh and blood
As if in sleeping he lay.

473

"Alas," said Bors, "That I was born
To ever see this indeed!
The best knight now his life has lost
That ever in battle rode steed!
Jesus, that crowned was with thorn,
In heaven his soul foster and feed!"
Then til the fifth day in the morn
They left him not to sing or read.

474

And then they made for him a bier,
The bishop and these others bold,
And from the chapel they did fare
To Joyous Gard that rich stronghold;
In the choir in a chapel there
A grave they made as they said they would,
And for three days kept their vigil there
In the castle with hearts so cold.

475

And as they stood around the bier
To bury him they had themselves brought,
In came Sir Ector his brother dear,
Who for seven years had him sought.
He looked into the choir there,
To hear a mass there he had thought
But all of them in such rapture were
They knew him and he them nought.

476

Sir Bors then did weep and sing
When that fair knight he did behold,
And every one his hands did wring,
The bishop and the others bold.
Sir Ector then asked them one thing
To know who this corpse was he would;
A hundred times his heart was near broke
When Sir Bors to him the tale told.

477

Bors courteously to him spake,
And to him he then said this:
"Here lies my lord Lancelot du Lake
For whom we sadly mourn like this."
Then Ector in his arms did take
The dead body to clasp and kiss,
And prayed all night he might watch make
For love of Jesus, King of Bliss.

478

Ector out of his wits near went
He wrung his hands like one gone mad;
So woefully did he lament
From all the sorrow that he had;
When over the corpse in his arms he bent
From out of his eyes the tears ran.
Then to their sorry work they went
And buried him with mood so sad.

479

Then on their knees they kneeled them down,
In truth it was a dolesome sight.
"From Jesus Christ I ask a boon,
And from His Mother, Mary bright;
Lord, as Thou made both sun and moon,
And as God and Man Thou are most of might,
Bring this soul unto Thy throne,
If ever Thou pitied a gentle knight."

480

Sir Ector went not to his steed,
He knew not whether to go or stay;
Then he chose to stay, there his life to lead
And for Lancelot all his life to pray.
He garbed him in a hermit's weed,
And to their chapel they went their way.
For a fortnight on foot their way they made
Ere home they came, truth to say.

481

When they came to Almsbury
Dead they found Gaynor the queen,
With color rosy and red as cherry,
And forth they bore her them between
And buried her with mass so merry
By King Arthur who had her husband been.
And now their chapel Glastonbury
Is an abbey rich of an order clean.

482

Of Lancelot du Lake I tell no more,
And thus I leave these hermits seven.
But still is Arthur buried there
And so too is Gaynor the queen
With these monks that are rich in lore.
And with voices mild they sing forever:
"Jesus, That suffered wounds so sore,
Grant us all the bliss of heaven."
                  Amen.

Here ends the Death of Arthur

BIBLIOGRAPHY

Benson, Larry D., ed. <u>King Arthur's Death</u>. Indianapolis, New York: Bobbs-Merrill Co., 1974.

Cable, James, trans. <u>The Death of King Arthur</u> (La Mort le Roi Artu). Middlesex, England: Penguin Books, 1971 – Reprint 1980.

Loomis, Roger Sherman, ed. <u>Arthurian Literature in the Middle Ages</u>. Oxford: Clarendon Press, 1959 – Reprint 1979.

Malory, Sir Thomas. <u>Le Morte D'Arthur</u>. 2 vol. ed. Janet Cowan. Middlesex, England: Penguin Books, 1969 – Reprint 1982.

Rhys, Ernest, ed. <u>Morte Arthur</u>. London, New York: Everyman's Library, 1912 – Reprint 1936.

Books of Related Interest

Cromwell's Press Agent: A Critical Biography of Marchamont Nedham, 1620-1678
   Joseph Frank, University of Massachusetts, Amherst

A Due Sense of Differences: An Evaluative Approach to Canadian Literature
   Wilfred Cude, Concordia University at Montreal

The Flight from Women in the Fiction of Saul Bellow
   Joseph F. McCadden, Burlington County College

Jane Austen and Samuel Johnson
   Peter L. DeRose, Lamar University

A Middle English Treatise on the Playing of Miracles
   Clifford Davidson, Western Michigan University

Passing the Love of Women: A Study of Gide's **Saul** *and its Biblical Roots*
   Anne Lapidus Lerner, Jewish Theological Seminary

Realism in Shakespeare's Romantic Comedies: "O Heavenly Mingle"
   Marvin Felheim, University of Michigan; Philip Traci, Wayne State University

The Search For An Eternal Norm: As Represented by Three Classics
   Louis J. Halle, Graduate Institute of International Studies, Geneva

Stephen Crane at Brede: An Anglo-American Literary Circle of the 1890's
   Gordon Milne, Lake Forest College

0-8191-5427-